Louis XIV

(John S. C. Abbott)

KARTINDO PUBLISHING HOUSE (Kartindo.Com)

PREFACE

We all live a double life: the external life which the world sees, and the internal life of hopes and fears, joys and griefs, temptations and sins, which the world sees not, and of which it knows but little. None lead this double life more emphatically than those who are seated upon thrones.

Though this historic sketch contains allusions to all the most important events in the reign of Louis XIV., it has been the main object of the writer to develop the inner life of the palace; to lead the reader into the interior of the Louvre, the Tuileries, Versailles, and Marly, and to exhibit the monarch as a man, in the details of domestic privacy.

This can more easily be done in reference to Louis XIV. than any other king. Very many of the prominent members of his household left their autobiographies, filled with the minutest incidents of every-day life.

It is impossible to give any correct idea of the life of this proud monarch without allusion to the corruption in the midst of which he spent his days. Still, the writer, while faithful to fact, has endeavored so to describe these scenes that any father can safely read the narrative aloud to his family.

There are few chapters in history more replete with horrors than that which records the "Revocation of the Edict of Nantes." The facts given are beyond all possibility of contradiction. In the contemplation of these scenes the mind pauses, bewildered by the reflection forced upon it, that many of the actors in these fiend-like outrages were inspired by motives akin to sincerity and conscientiousness.

The thoughtful reader will perceive that in this long and wicked reign Louis XIV. was sowing the wind from which his descendants reaped the whirlwind. It was the despotism of Louis XIV. and of Louis XV. which ushered in that most sublime of all earthly dramas, the French Revolution.

JOHN S. C. ABBOTT.

New Haven, Conn., 1870.

KARTINDO PUBLISHING HOUSE (Kartindo.Com)

CONTENTS

KARTINDO PUBLISHING HOUSE (Kartindo.Com)

CHAPTER I

BIRTH AND CHILDHOOD

1615-1650

Marriage of Louis XIII.--Character of Louis XIII.--Character of Anne of Austria.--Cardinal Richelieu.--The Duke of Buckingham.--His death.-- Estrangement of the king and queen.--Joy of the nation.--Birth of Louis XIV.-- Gift of the Pope.--Condition of Paris.--Reconciliation of the king and queen.-- Orders of Louis XIII. respecting the dauphin.--Ill health of Louis XIII.--The dauphin declared King Louis XIV.--Last hours of Louis XIII.--Death of Louis XIII.--Louis XIV. recognized king.--Palais Royal.--Apartments of the queen regent.--Educational arrangements for Louis XIV.--Speech of Louis at five years old.--Dislikes the change of teachers.--Interest in history.--Mazarin's wicked policy.--Henrietta, queen of Charles I.--Figure and bearing of the king.- -His first campaign.--The cardinal's nieces.--Anecdote.--Feud between Mazarin and the Parliament.--Alarm of Mazarin.--Escape of the royal family from Paris.--Flight of the court.--Discomfort of the court at St. Germain.-- Excitement in Paris.--Issue of a parliamentary decree.--Origin of the names Fronde and Mazarins.--Two rival courts.--Straw scarce.--Character of Mazarin.--Termination of the war.--Society reversed.

Louis XIII. of France married Anne of Austria on the 25th of November, 1615. The marriage ceremony was performed with great splendor in the Cathedral of Bordeaux. The bride was exceedingly beautiful, tall, and of exquisite proportions. She possessed the whitest and most delicate hand that ever made an imperious gesture. Her eyes were of matchless beauty, easily dilated, and of extraordinary transparency. Her small and ruddy mouth looked like an opening rose-bud. Long and silky hair, of a lovely shade of auburn, gave to the face it surrounded the sparkling complexion of a blonde, and the animation of a brunette.[A]

[Footnote A: Louis XIV. et son Siècle.]

The marriage was not a happy one. Louis XIII. was not a man of any mental or physical attractions. He was cruel, petulant, and jealous. The king had a younger brother, Gaston, duke of Anjou. He was a young man of joyous spirits, social, frank, a universal favorite. His moody, taciturn brother did not love him. Anne did. She could not but enjoy his society. Wounded by the coldness and neglect of her husband, it is said that she was not unwilling, by rather a free exhibition of the fascinations of her person and her mind, to win the admiration of Gaston. She hoped thus to inspire the king with a more just appreciation of her merits.

Louis XIII., at the time of his marriage, was a mere boy fourteen years of age. His father had died when he was nine years old. He was left under the care of his mother, Mary de Medicis, as regent. Anne of Austria was a maturely developed and precocious child of eleven years when she gave her hand to the boy-king of France. Not much discretion could have been expected of two such children, exposed to the idleness, the splendors, and the corruption of a court.

Anne was vain of her beauty, naturally coquettish, and very romantic in her views of life. It is said that the queen dowager, wishing to prevent Anne from gaining much influence over the mind of the king, did all she could to lure her into flirtations and gallantries, which alienated her from her husband. For this purpose she placed near her person Madame Chevreuse, an intriguing woman, alike renowned for wit, beauty, and unscrupulousness.

Quite a desperate flirtation arose between Anne and little Gaston, who was but nine years of age. Gaston, whom the folly of the times entitled Duke of Anjou, hated Louis, and delighted to excite his jealousy and anger by his open and secret manifestation of love for the beautiful Anne. The king's health failed. He became increasingly languid, morose, emaciate. Anne, young as she was, was physically a fully developed woman of voluptuous beauty. The undisguised alienation which existed between her and the king encouraged other courtiers of eminent rank to court her smiles.

Cardinal Richelieu, notwithstanding his ecclesiastical vows, became not only the admirer, but the lover of the queen, addressing her in the most impassioned words of endearment. Thus years of intrigue and domestic wretchedness passed away until 1624. The queen had then been married nine years, and was twenty years of age. She had no children.

The reckless, hot-headed George Villiers, duke of Buckingham, visited the French court to arrange terms of marriage between Henrietta Maria, sister of Louis XIII., and the Prince of Wales, son of James I. of England. He was what is called a splendid man, of noble bearing, and of chivalric devotion to the fair.

KARTINDO PUBLISHING HOUSE (Kartindo.Com)

The duke, boundlessly rich, displayed great magnificence in Paris. He danced with the queen, fascinated her by his openly avowed admiration, and won such smiles in return as to induce the king and Cardinal Richelieu almost to gnash their teeth with rage.

This flirtation, if we may not express it by a more emphatic phrase, created much heart-burning and wretchedness, criminations and recriminations, in the regal palace. In August, 1628, the Duke of Buckingham, then in England, terminated his wretched and guilty life. He fell beneath the dagger of an assassin. Anne, disdaining all dissimulation, wept openly, and, secluding herself from the gayeties of the court, surrendered herself to grief.

A mutual spirit of defiance existed between the king and queen. Both were wretched. Such are always the wages of sin. Ten more joyless years passed away. The rupture between the royal pair was such that they could scarcely endure each other. Louis himself was the first to inform the queen of the news so satisfactory to him, so heart-rending to her, that a dagger had pierced the heart of Buckingham. After this they met only at unfrequent intervals. All confidence and sympathy were at an end. It was a bitter disappointment to the queen that she had no children. Upon the death of the king, who was in very feeble health, her own position and influence would depend almost entirely upon her having a son to whom the crown would descend. Louis resided generally at the Castle of Blois. Anne held her court at the Louvre.

A married life of twenty-two years had passed away, and still the queen had no child. Both she and her husband had relinquished all hope of offspring. On the evening of the 5th of December, 1637, the king, having made a visit to the Convent of the Visitation, being overtaken by a storm, drove to the Louvre instead of Blois. He immediately proceeded to the apartments of the queen. Anne was astonished, and did not disguise her astonishment at seeing him. He, however, remained until the morrow.

[Illustration: THE CASTLE OF BLOIS.]

Soon after this, to the inexpressible joy of the queen, it appeared that she was to become a mother. The public announcement of the fact created surprise and joy throughout the nation. The king was equally astonished and delighted. He immediately hastened to the Louvre to offer the queen his congratulations.

The queen repaired to St. Germain-en-Laye, about six miles from Versailles, to

KARTINDO PUBLISHING HOUSE (Kartindo.Com)

await the birth of her child. Here she occupied, in the royal palace, the gorgeous apartments in which Henry IV. had formerly dwelt. The king himself also took up his abode in the palace. The excitement was so great that St. Germain was crowded with the nobility, who had flocked to the place in anxious expectancy of the great event. Others, who could not be accommodated at St. Germain, stationed couriers on the road to obtain the earliest intelligence of the result.

On the 5th of September, 1638, the king was greeted with the joyful tidings of the birth of a son. A vast crowd had assembled in front of the palace. The king, in the exuberance of his delight, took the child from the nurse, and, stepping out upon a balcony, exhibited him to the crowd, exclaiming, "A son! gentlemen, a son!"

The announcement was received with a universal shout of joy. The happy father then took the babe into an adjoining apartment, where the bishops were assembled to perform the ordinance of baptism. These dignitaries of the Church had been kneeling around a temporary altar praying for the queen. The Bishop of Meaux performed the ceremony. A Te Deum was then chanted in the chapel of the castle. Immediately after this, the king wrote an autograph letter to the corporation of Paris, announcing the joyful tidings. A courier was dispatched with the document at his highest possible speed.

The enthusiasm excited in the capital surpassed any thing which had ever before been witnessed. The common people, the nobles, the ecclesiastics, and the foreign embassadors, vied with each other in their demonstrations of joy. A few months after, in July, an extraordinary messenger arrived from the pope, to convey to the august mother and her child the blessing of the holy father. He also presented the queen, for her babe, swaddling-clothes which had been blessed by his holiness. These garments were exceedingly rich with gold and silver embroidery. They were inclosed in a couple of chests of red velvet, and elicited the admiration of the royal pair.

The France of that day was very different from that magnificent empire which now stands in intellectual culture, arts, and arms, prominent among the nations of the globe. The country was split up into hostile factions, over which haughty nobles ruled. The roads in the rural districts were almost impassable. Paris itself was a small and dirty city, with scarcely any police regulations, and infested with robbers. There were no lamps to light the city by night. The streets were narrow, ill paved, and choked with mud and refuse. Immediately after nightfall these dark and crooked thoroughfares were thronged with robbers and assassins, whose depredations were of the most audacious kind.

Socially, morally, and intellectually, France was at the lowest ebb. The masses of the people were in a degraded condition of squalid poverty and debasement. Still the king, by enormous taxation, succeeded in wresting from his wretched subjects an income to meet the expenses of his court, amounting to about four millions of our money. But the outlays were so enormous that even this income was quite unavailing, and innumerable measures of extortion were adopted to meet the deficit.

The king was so much gratified by the birth of a dauphin that for a time he became quite reconciled to his beautiful and haughty queen. Two years after the birth of the dauphin, on the 21st of September, 1640, Anne gave birth to a second son, who took the title of Philip, duke of Anjou. The queen and her two children resided in the beautiful palace of Saint Germain-en-Laye, where the princes were born.

A company of French Guards, commanded by Captain Montigni, protected the castle. Madame de Lausac was the governess of the two children. The title by which the king's brother was usually designated was simply Monsieur. But for these children of the king, the crown, upon the death of the monarch, would descend immediately to Monsieur, the king's brother. The morals of the times were such that the king was ever apprehensive that some harm might come to the children through the intrigues of his brother. Monsieur lived in Paris. The king left orders with Madame de Lausac that, should his brother visit the queen, the officers of the household should immediately surround the dauphin for his protection, and that Monsieur should not be permitted to enter the palace should he be accompanied by more than three persons.

[Illustration: PALACE OF SAINT GERMAIN-EN-LAYE.]

To Montigni, the captain of the guard, the king gave half of a gold coin, of which he retained the other half. Montigni was commanded to watch over the persons of the princes with the utmost vigilance. Should he receive an order to remove them, or to transfer them to other hands, he was enjoined not to obey that order, even should it be in the handwriting of his majesty himself, unless he at the same time received the other half of the broken coin.

The king, as we have mentioned, had been for some time in feeble health. Early in the spring of 1643 he became seriously ill. The symptoms were so alarming as to lead the king, as well as his friends, to think that death could not be far distant. There are few men so hardened as to be able to contemplate without some degree of anxiety death and the final judgment. The king was alarmed. He betook himself to prayer and to the scrupulous discharge of his religious duties.

In preparation for the great change, he repaired to Saint Germain to invest the queen with the regency when he should die. His brother, Monsieur, who had taken the title of the Duke of Orleans, and all the leading nobles of the court, were present. The king, pale, emaciate, and with death staring him in the face, was bolstered in his bed. Anne of Austria stood weeping by his side. She did not love her husband--she did love power; but the scene was so solemn and so affecting as to force tears into all eyes. The dauphin was then four and a half years old. He was declared king, with the title of Louis XIV., under the regency of his mother until he should attain his majority.

The next day, April 21st, the christening of the dauphin with his new title took place with great state in the chapel of the palace. After the celebration of the rite, the dauphin was carried into the chamber of his dying father, and seated upon the bed by his side. The poor king, dying in the prime of life, was oppressed with the profoundest melancholy. There was nothing in the memory of the past to give him pleasure; nothing in the future to inspire him with well-grounded hope. Turning to the little prince, who had just been christened with the royal title, he inquired,

"What is your name, my child?"

"Louis XIV.," the dauphin promptly replied.

"Not yet," said the king, sadly, shaking his head; "but pray God that it may soon be so."

A few more days of sickness and suffering passed away, during which it was almost hourly expected that the king would die. Death often comes to the palace invested with terrors unknown in the cottage. Beneath his sceptre all gradations and conditions of rank disappear. The sufferings of the king were such that he longed for release.

On the 13th of May, as the shades of evening were gathering around his dying bed, he anxiously inquired of his physicians if it were possible that he could live until morning. They consulted together, and then informed him that they did not think it possible.

"God be praised!" the king replied. "I think it is now time that I should take leave of all whom I love."

The royal household was immediately assembled around the couch of the dying monarch. He had sufficient strength to throw his arms around the neck of the queen, and to press her tenderly to his heart. In such an hour past differences are forgotten. In low and broken tones of voice, the king addressed the queen in a few parting words of endearment.

The dauphin was then placed in his arms. Silently, but with tearful eyes, he pressed his thin and parched lips to both cheeks and to the brow of the child, who was too young to comprehend the solemn import of the scene.

His brother, Monsieur, the duke of Orleans, the king had never loved. In these later years he had regarded him with implacable hostility. But, subdued by the influences of death, he bade that brother an eternal adieu, with even fond caresses. Indeed, he had become so far reconciled to Monsieur that he had appointed him lieutenant general of the kingdom, under the regency of Anne of Austria, during the minority of the dauphin.

Several of the higher ecclesiastics were present, who had assisted in preparing him to die. He affectionately embraced them all, and then requested the Bishop of Meaux to read the service for the dying. While it was being read he sank into a lethargy, and never spoke again. He died in the forty-second year of his age, after a reign of thirty-three years, having ascended the throne when but nine years old.

Immediately after the death of the king, Anne of Austria held a private interview with Monsieur, in which they agreed to co-operate in the maintenance of each other's authority. The Parliament promptly recognized the queen as regent, and the Duke of Orleans as lieutenant general, during the minority of the dauphin.

The Duke de Grammont, one of the highest nobles of France, and a distinguished member of the court of Louis XIII., had a son, the Count de Guiche, a few months older than the dauphin. This child was educated as the play-fellow and the companion in study of the young king. One of the first acts of Anne of Austria was to assemble the leading bodies of the realm to take the oath of allegiance to her son. The little fellow, four and a half years old, arrayed in imperial robes, was seated upon the throne. The Count de Guiche, a very sedate, thoughtful, precocious child, was placed upon the steps, that his undoubted propriety of behavior might be a pattern to the infant king. Both of the children behaved remarkably well.

Soon after this, at the close of the year 1643, the queen, with her household, who had resided during the summer in the palace of the Louvre, took up her residence in what was then called the Cardinal Palace. This magnificent building, which had been reared at an enormous expense, had been bequeathed by the Cardinal Richelieu to the young king. But it was suggested that it was not decorous that the king should inhabit a mansion which bore the name of the residence of a subject. Therefore the inscription of *Cardinal Palace* was effaced from above the doorway, and that of *Palais Royal* placed in its stead. The palace had cost the cardinal a sum nearly equal to a million of dollars. This ungrateful disregard of the memory of the cardinal greatly displeased his surviving friends, and called forth earnest remonstrance. But all expostulations were in vain. From that day to this the renowned mansion has been known only as the "Palais Royal." The opposite engraving shows the palace as left by the cardinal. Since his day the building has been greatly enlarged by extending the wings for shops around the whole inclosure of the garden.

Louis XIV. was at this time five years old. The apartments which had been occupied by Richelieu were assigned to the dauphin. His mother, the queen regent, selected for herself rooms far more spacious and elegant. Though they were furnished and embellished with apparently every appliance of luxury, Anne, fond of power and display, expended enormous sums in adapting them to her taste. The cabinet of the regent, in the gorgeousness of its adornments, was considered the wonder of Paris.

[Illustration: THE PALAIS ROYAL.]

Cardinal Mazarin had also a suite of rooms assigned him in the palace which looked out upon the Rue des bons Enfans. These households were quite distinct, and they were all surrounded with much of the pageantry of royalty. The superintendence of the education of the young prince was intrusted to the cardinal. He had also his governor, his sub-governor, his preceptor, and his valet de chambre, each of whom must have occupied posts of honor rather than of responsibility. The Marchioness de Senecey, and other ladies of high rank, were intrusted with the special care of the dauphin until he should attain the age of seven years.

Thus the court of the baby-king was quite imposing. From his earliest years he was accustomed to the profoundest homage, and was trained to the most rigid rules of etiquette. The dauphin early developed a fondness for military exercises. Very eagerly he shouldered the musket, brandished the sword, and beat the drum. The temperament of his brother Philip, the duke of Anjou, was very different: he was remarkably gentle, quiet, and affectionate. Gradually the baby-court of the dauphin was increased by the addition of other lads. The young king was the central luminary around whom they all revolved. By them all the dauphin was regarded with a certain kind of awe, as if he were a being of a superior, almost of a celestial race. These lads were termed "children of honor." They always addressed the king, and were addressed in return, with the formality of full-grown men. One day a little fellow named Lomenie delighted the king with a gift. The king was amusing himself with a cross-bow, which for the time being happened to be in special favor. He loaned the bow for a few moments to Lomenie. Soon, however, anxious to regain the valued plaything, he held out his hand to take it back. His governess, the Marchioness de Senecey, said to him, aside,

"Sire, kings give what they lend."

Louis, immediately approaching his companion, said, calmly, "Monsieur de Lomenie, keep the cross-bow. I wish that it were something of more importance; but, such as it is, I give it to you with all my heart."

This was a speech of a boy of five years old to a companion of the same age. When the dauphin reached his seventh birthday, a great change took place in his household. All his female attendants were withdrawn, and he was placed exclusively under the charge of men. It is said that this change was at first the occasion of much grief to him. He had become much attached to many of the ladies, who had devoted themselves to the promotion of his happiness. We are told that he was greatly chagrined to find that none of the gentlemen of his court could tell him any of those beautiful fairy tales with which the ladies had often lulled him to sleep. In conference with the queen upon the subject, it was decided that M. Laporte, his first valet de chambre, should read to him every night a chapter of a very popular history of France. The dauphin soon became greatly interested in the narrative. He declared that he, when he grew up, would be a Charlemagne, a St. Louis, a Francis First, and expressed great abhorrence of the tyrannical and slothful kings.

The pleasure which the little king took in these historical readings daily increased. Cardinal Mazarin accidentally found out what was going on, and was greatly displeased. He was anxious that the intellectual powers of the king should not be developed, for the cardinal desired to grasp the reins of government with his own hands. To do this, it was necessary that the king should be kept ignorant, and should be incited only to enervating indulgence.

Scornfully the cardinal remarked, "I presume the governor of the king must put on his shoes and stockings, as I perceive his valet de chambre is teaching him history."

The young king entertained an instinctive aversion to the proud cardinal, who assumed imperial airs, and who was living in splendor far surpassing that of the regent or of the child-king. Those who surrounded the prince were equally inimical to the cardinal-minister, who, in that age of superstition and fanaticism, had attained such power that the regent herself stood in awe of him.

Henrietta, queen of England, wife of the unfortunate Charles I., was a daughter of Henry IV., and sister of Louis XIII. She was consequently aunt to the dauphin. The troubles in England, which soon led to the beheading of the king her husband, rendered it necessary for her to escape to France. Her brother, Monsieur, duke of Orleans, went to the coast to receive his unhappy and royal sister. As they approached Paris, the queen regent and her son the king rode out to meet them. Henrietta took a seat in the same carriage with their majesties, and returned with them to the Louvre. The pallid cheeks and saddened features of the English queen proclaimed so loudly the woes with which she was stricken as to exert universal sympathy.

The young king at seven years of age was tall, muscular, and excelled in all physical exercises; but the villainous cardinal had endeavored in every way to dwarf his intellect, so that his mind remained almost a blank. Both the young king and his brother at this early age had acquired a very remarkable degree of courtly grace. A chronicler of the times, speaking of the bearing of Louis at a court wedding, says,

"The king, with the gracefulness which shines in all his actions, took the hand of the Queen of Poland, and conducted her to the platform, where his majesty opened the dance, and was followed by nearly all the princes, princesses, great nobles, and ladies of the court. At its termination, the king, with the same grace and majestic deportment, conducted the young queen to her place. The king then danced a second time, and led out the Duke of Anjou with such skill that every one was charmed with the polite bearing of these two young princes."

Early in the year 1646, the king, not yet quite eight years old, was conducted upon what was singularly called his first campaign. The queen and her son repaired to Amiens, where they sojourned for a short time with the army, and established a very brilliant court. When the army left Amiens for Flanders, the regent and her son returned from their campaign.

The infant court of the monarch was now established at Paris. The ambitious cardinal had brought from Italy several little children, his relatives, the eldest of whom had attained but her twelfth year. They were immediately introduced to the court of Louis XIV. The wealth of the cardinal was such, and his influence so great, that, young as these his nieces were, they were instantly surrounded by admirers. The Duke of Orleans, who hated the cardinal and all that belonged to him, bitterly remarked,

"There is such a throng about those little girls that I doubt if their lives are safe, and if they will not be suffocated."

The boy-king, however, notwithstanding his dislike for the cardinal, received the little girls with that gallantry for which throughout life he was distinguished.

Very early he began to develop quite a positive character. On one occasion the courtiers were speaking in his presence of the absolute power exercised by the sultans of Turkey. Several very striking examples were given. The young prince, who had listened attentively, remarked,

"That is as it should be; that is really reigning."

"Yes, sire," pertinently replied Marshal d'Estrées, "but two or three of those sultans have, within my memory, been strangled."

The Prince de Condé inquired of Laporte, the first valet of the king, respecting the character his young majesty was developing. Upon being told that he was conscientious and intelligent, he replied, "So much the better. There would be no pleasure in obeying a fool, and no honor in being commanded by a bad man."

KARTINDO PUBLISHING HOUSE (Kartindo.Com)

Cardinal Mazarin, the prime minister, who looked with jealousy upon any development of superior intelligence in the dauphin, said to Marshal de Grammont, "Ah! sir, you do not know his majesty. There is enough stuff in him to make four kings and an honest man."

There had gradually sprung up a deadly feud between the court, headed by the tyrannical minister Mazarin on the one side, and by the Parliament on the other. The populace of Paris were in sympathy with the Parliament. Many of the prominent nobles, some even of royal blood, detesting the haughty prime minister, espoused the Parliamentary cause. There were riots in Paris. Affairs looked very threatening. Mazarin was alarmed, and decided to escape from Paris with the court to the palace of St. Germain. There he could protect the court with an ample military force. He thought, also, that he should be able to cut off the supply of provisions from the capital, and thus starve the city into subjection.

It was necessary to move with much caution, as the people were greatly agitated, were filling the streets with surging crowds, and would certainly prevent the removal of the king should they suspect the design. The night of the 5th of January was selected as a time in which to attempt the escape. The matter was kept profoundly secret from most of the members of the royal household.

At three o'clock in the morning a carriage was drawn up in the gate of the royal garden. The queen regent, who, to avoid suspicion, had retired to bed at the usual hour, had in the mean time risen and was prepared for her flight. The young king and his brother were awoke from their sleep, hurriedly dressed, and conveyed to the carriage in waiting. The queen regent, with several other prominent members of the court, descended the back stairs which led from the queen's apartment and joined the children. Immediately one or two other carriages drove up, and the whole party entered them, and by different routes, through the dark and narrow streets, left the city. It was a short ride of about twelve miles.

Other prominent members of the court, residing in different parts of the city, had been apprised of the movement, so that at five o'clock in the morning twenty carriages, containing one hundred and fifty persons, drove into the court-yard of the palace. One of the ladies who accompanied the expedition, Mademoiselle Montpensier, gives the following graphic description of the scene:

"When we arrived at St. Germain we went straight to the chapel to hear mass. All the rest of the day was spent in questioning those who arrived as to what they were doing in Paris. The drums were beating all over the city, and the citizens had taken up arms. The Countess de Fiesque sent me a coach, and a mattress, and a little linen. As I was in so sorry a condition, I went to seek help at the Chateau Neuf, where *Monsieur and Madame* were lodged; but Madame had not her clothes any more than myself. Nothing could be more laughable than this disorder. I lodged in a large room, well painted and gilded, with but little fire, which is not agreeable in the month of January. My mattress was laid upon the floor, and my sister, who had no bed, slept with me. Judge if I were agreeably situated for a person who had slept but little the previous night, with sore throat and violent cold.

"Fortunately for me, the beds of Monsieur and Madame arrived. Monsieur had the kindness to give me the room which he vacated. As I was in the apartment of Monsieur, where no one knew that I was lodged, I was awoke by a noise. I drew back my curtain, and was much astonished to find my chamber quite filled by men in large buff skin collars, who appeared surprised to see me, and who knew me as little as I knew them.

"I had no change of linen, and my day chemise was washed during the night. I had no women to arrange my hair and dress me, which is very inconvenient. I ate with Monsieur, who keeps a very bad table. Still I did not lose my gayety, and Monsieur was in admiration at my making no complaint. It is true I am a creature who can make the best of every thing, and am greatly above trifles. I remained in this state ten days, at the end of which time my equipage arrived, and I was very glad to have all my comforts. I then went to lodge in the chateau Vieux, where the queen was residing."[B]

[Footnote B: There were at that time two palaces at St. Germain. The old palace, originally built by Charles V., and in the alteration of which Louis XIV. spent over a million of dollars, still remains. The new palace, constructed by Henry IV. about a quarter of a mile from the other, is now in ruins.]

At a very early hour in the morning the news was circulated through the streets of Paris that the court had fled from the city, taking with it the young king. The excitement was terrible, creating universal shouts and tumults. All who were in any way connected with the court attempted to escape in various disguises to join the royal party. The populace, on the other hand, closed the gates, and barricaded the streets, to prevent their flight. In the midst of this confusion, a letter was received by the municipal magistrates, over the signature of the boy-king, stating that he had been compelled to leave the capital to prevent the seizure of his person by the Parliament, and urging the magistrates to do all in their power for the preservation of order and for the protection of property. The king also ordered the Parliament immediately to retire from the city to Montargis.

The Parliament refused to recognize the order, declaring "that it did not emanate from the monarch himself, but from the evil counselors by whom he was held in captivity." Upon the reception of this reply, the queen regent, who had surrounded her palace at St. Germain with a thousand royal troops, acting under the guidance of Mazarin, issued a decree forbidding the villages around Paris sending into the capital either bread, wine, or cattle. Troops were also stationed to cut off such supplies. This attempt to subdue the people by the terrors of famine excited intense exasperation. A decree was promptly issued by the Parliament stating,

"Since Cardinal Mazarin is notoriously the author of the present troubles, the Parliament declares him to be the disturber of the public peace, the enemy of the king and the state, and orders him to retire from the court in the course of this day, and in eight days more from the kingdom. Should he neglect to do this, at the expiration of the appointed time all the subjects of the king are called upon to hunt him down."

At the same time, men-at-arms were levied in sufficient numbers to escort safely into the city all those who would bring in provisions. The Parliament, from the populace of Paris, could bring sixty thousand bayonets upon any field of battle. Thus very serious civil war was inaugurated.

As we have mentioned, many of the nobles, some of whom were allied to the royal family, assuming that they were not contending against their legitimate sovereign, the young king, but against the detested Mazarin, were in cordial co-operation with the Parliament. The people in the rural districts were also in sympathy with the party in Paris.

The court party was now called "The *Mazarins*," and those of the Parliament "The *Fronde*." The literal meaning of the word fronde is sling. It is a boy's plaything, and when skillfully used, an important weapon of war. It was with the sling that David slew Goliath. During the Middle Ages this was the usual weapon of the foot soldiers. Mazarin had contemptuously remarked that the Parliament were like school boys, *fronding in the ditches*, and who ran away at the approach of a policeman. The Parliament accepted the title, and adopted the *fronde* or *sling* as the emblem of their party.

There were now two rival courts in France. The one at St. Germain was in a state of great destitution. The palace was but partially furnished, and not at all capable of affording comfortable accommodations for the crowd which thronged its apartments. Nothing could be obtained from Paris. Their purses were empty. The rural population was hostile, and, while eager to carry their products to Paris, were unwilling to bring them to St. Germain. Madame de Motteville states in her memoirs "that the king, queen, and cardinal were sleeping upon straw, which soon became so scarce that it could not be obtained for money."

The court of the Fronde was assembled at the Hotel de Ville in Paris. There all was splendor, abundance, festive enjoyment. The high rank of the leaders and the beauty of the ladies gave éclat to the gathering.

Cardinal Mazarin was not only extortionate, but miserly. He had accumulated an enormous property. All this was seized and appropriated by the Fronde. Though there were occasional skirmishes between the forces of the two factions, neither of them seemed disposed to plunge into the horrors of civil war.

The king sent a herald, clad in complete armor and accompanied by two trumpeters, to the Parliament. The Fronde refused to receive the herald, but decided to send a deputation to the king to ascertain what overtures he was willing to make. After a lengthy conference a not very satisfactory compromise was agreed upon, and the royal fugitives returned to Paris. It was the 5th of April, 1650. A Te Deum was chanted with great pomp at the cathedral of Notre Dame.

"Thus terminated the first act of the most singular, bootless, and, we are almost tempted to add, burlesque war which, in all probability, Europe ever witnessed. Throughout its whole duration society appeared to have been smitten with some moral hallucination. Kings and cardinals slept on mattresses, princesses and duchesses on straw. Market-women embraced princes, prelates governed armies, court ladies led the mob, and the mob, in its turn, ruled the city."[C]

[Footnote C: Louis XIV. and the Court of France, vol. i., p, 262.]

KARTINDO PUBLISHING HOUSE (Kartindo.Com)

CHAPTER II

THE BOY-KING

1650-1653

M. de Retz.--Fears of Mazarin.--Escape of the cardinal.--Dangers of civil war.--Alarm and energy of De Retz.--The populace aroused.--Palace of the Luxembourg.--Discovery of the attempted flight of the royal family.--Haughty reply of Anne of Austria.--Courage of the queen mother.--Respectful conduct of the populace.--Fortitude of the regent.--The queen regent dissembles.--Vigilance of Monsieur.--Cardinal Mazarin in exile.--Majority of the dauphin attained.--Imposing ceremony.--Appearance of Louis XIV.--Address of Louis.--Address of the queen regent.--Reply of Louis.--Power of the King of France.--Gallantry of Louis.--Influence of Anne and Mazarin upon Louis.--Conflict between the court and Parliament.--Mazarin arrives in France.--Civil war inaugurated.--Mazarin's army defeated.--Depression of the regent.--*Monsieur.*--Ludicrous quarrel of Louis and his brother.--Embarrassment of the court.--Conflict at Etampes.--Destitution of Louis XIV.--Scenes of the conflict at Etampes.--Retreat of Condé.--Battle at St. Antoine.--Cardinal Mazarin forced to retire.--The king invited to return.--The Duke of Orleans retires to Blois.--Doom of the leaders of the Fronde.--Respectful refusal of De Retz.--Orders for his arrest.--Treachery of Anne of Austria.--Arrest of De Retz.--Return of Mazarin.--First care of Mazarin.--Festivities at court.--Approaching coronation.--Paucity of notabilities at the coronation.--The king repairs to Stenay.--Louis in the trenches.--Defeat of Condé.

The reconciliation between the court and the Fronde was very superficial. The old antagonism soon reappeared, and daily grew more rancorous. To add to the embarrassment of the court, *Monsieur*, the duke of Orleans, became alienated from Mazarin, and seemed inclined to join the Fronde. The most formidable antagonist of the cardinal in the Parliament was M. de Retz. He was coadjutor of the Archbishop of Paris, a man of consummate address and great powers of eloquence.

The struggle between De Retz and Mazarin soon became one of life and death. The coadjutor was at length imboldened to offer a decree in Parliament urging the king to banish from his presence and his councils Cardinal Mazarin. This measure threw the court into consternation. The cardinal was apprehensive of arrest. Some of his friends urged him to retire immediately to a fortress. Others proposed to garrison the Palais Royal and its neighborhood with an efficient guard.

From the saloons of the palace the shouts were heard of the excited populace swarming through the streets. No one could tell to what extremes of violence they might proceed. Warned by these hostile demonstrations, the cardinal decided to escape from Paris. At ten o'clock at night he took leave of the queen regent, hastened to his apartments, exchanged his ecclesiastical costume for a dress in which he was entirely disguised, and on foot threaded the dark streets to escape from the city. Two of his friends accompanied him. At the Richelieu Gate they took horses, which were awaiting them there, and in two hours alighted at the palace of St. Germain.

M. de Retz, through his spies, was immediately informed of the flight of the cardinal. He at once hastened to communicate the intelligence to *Monsieur*. The duke at first could not credit the statement, as he felt assured that Mazarin would not have left without taking the young king with him. Should the cardinal, in his retreat, gain possession of the king, in whose name he would issue all his orders, it would be hardly possible to avoid the horrors of a desolating civil war. All minds in Paris, from the highest to the lowest, were thrown into a state of the most intense excitement.

On the night of the second day after the cardinal's flight, M. de Retz was awakened by a messenger, who informed him that the Duke of Orleans was anxious to see him immediately at the palace of the Luxembourg. The coadjutor rose, hastily dressed, and in great anxiety repaired to the palace. The duke, though lieutenant general of the kingdom, was a very timid man, and exceedingly inefficient in action. As they entered the chamber of the duke, he listlessly said to M. de Retz,

"It is just as you said. The king is about to leave Paris; what shall we do? I do not see what can be done to prevent it."

The resolute coadjutor replied, "We must immediately take possession of the city gates."

But the inert and weak duke brought forward sundry silly excuses. He had not sufficient force of character or moral courage to commit himself to any decisive

KARTINDO PUBLISHING HOUSE (Kartindo.Com)

course of action. The only measure he could be induced to adopt was to send a message to the queen regent, imploring her to reflect upon the consequences which would inevitably result from the removal of the king from Paris. In the mean time, the resolute and fearless coadjutor sent his emissaries in all directions. The populace were aroused with the cry that Mazarin was about to carry off the king. The gates of the city were seized. Mounted patrols traversed the streets urging the citizens to arms. An enormous crowd of excited men and women rushed toward the Palais Royal.

[Illustration: PALACE OF THE LUXEMBOURG.]

The carriages were, in fact, at that hour, at the appointed rendezvous for the midnight flight of the king and his attendants. The young monarch was already in his traveling dress, just about to descend the stairs of the palace, when the queen was apprised, by the tumult in the streets, that the design was discovered, and that consequently its execution was impracticable.

With the utmost precipitancy, the traveling dress of the king was removed, and he was robed in his night garments, replaced in bed, and urged to feign that he was asleep. Scarcely was this accomplished ere one of the officers of the household entered and announced to the queen that the exasperated mob was threatening the palace, insisting upon seeing the king, that they might satisfy themselves that he had not been carried away. While he was speaking, another messenger entered with the announcement that the mob had already proceeded to violence, and were tearing down the palisades of the palace. While he was yet speaking, a messenger from the Duke of Orleans arrived, imploring the queen regent not to attempt the removal of the king, and assuring her that it was impossible to do so, since the citizens were resolved to prevent it.

The queen, with dignity, listened to all. To the messenger of the Duke of Orleans she haughtily replied,

"Say to the duke that he, instigated by the coadjutor, has caused this tumult, and that he has power to allay it. That nothing can be more unfounded than the idea that there has been any design to remove the king. That both his majesty and his brother, the Duke of Anjou, are asleep in their beds, as I myself had been until the uproar in the streets had caused me to rise." To satisfy the messenger, M. de Souches, she led him into the chamber of the king, and showed him his majesty apparently soundly asleep.

As they were softly retiring from the room, the outcry of the populace filling the court-yard was heard shouting "The king! the king! we must see the king." The queen regent hesitated for a moment, and then, with wonderful presence of mind, and with moral and physical courage rarely equaled, turning to the envoy of *Monsieur*, said,

"Say to the people that the doors of the palace shall be immediately thrown open, and that every one who wishes may enter the chamber of the king. But inform them that his majesty is asleep, and request them to be as quiet as is possible."

M. Souches obeyed. The doors were opened. The mob rushed in. Nevertheless, contrary to all expectation, they had no sooner reached the royal apartment than their leaders, remembering that their king was sleeping, desired the untimely visitors to proceed in perfect quiet. As the human tide moved onward, their very breathing was suppressed. They trod the floor with softest footsteps. The same tumultuous multitude that had howled, and yelled, and threatened outside the gates, now, in the chamber of the sovereign, became calm, respectful, and silent. They approached the royal bed with a feeling of affectionate deference, which restrained every intruder from drawing back the curtains.

The queen herself performed this office. She stood at the pillow of her son, beautiful in features, of queenly grace in form and stature. Pale, calm, and dignified as though she were performing some ordinary court ceremonial, she gathered back the folds of the velvet drapery, and revealed to the gaze of the people their young sovereign in all the beauty of youth, and apparently in profound slumber.

This living stream of men and women from the streets of Paris continued to flow through the chamber until three o'clock in the morning, entering at one door and passing out at its opposite. Through this trying scene the queen never faltered.

"Like a marble statue," writes Miss Pardoe, "she retained her position, firm and motionless, her majestic figure drawn haughtily to its full height, and her magnificent arm resting in broad relief upon the crimson draperies. And still the boy-king, emulating the example of his royal parent, remained immobile, with closed eyes and steady breathing, as though his rest had remained unbroken by the incursion of his rebellious subjects. It was a singular and marked passage in the life of both mother and son."[D]

KARTINDO PUBLISHING HOUSE (Kartindo.Com)

[Footnote D: Louis XIV. and the Court of France, vol. i., page 351.]

In those days and at that court falsehood was deemed an indispensable part of diplomacy. In the afternoon of the same day in which the scene we have described occurred, the queen assembled in her saloon in the palace the prominent magistrates of the city. With firm voice and undaunted eye, she assured them that she had never entertained the slightest idea of removing his majesty from the city. She enjoined it upon them vigilantly to continue to guard the gates, that the populace might be convinced that no design of escape was cherished. Her words were not believed; her directions were obeyed. The gates were rigidly closed. Thus the king was a prisoner.

The apprehensions of the Fronde, that by some stratagem the king might be removed, were so great that *Monsieur* dispatched a gentleman of his household every night to ascertain if the king were quietly in his bed. The messenger, M. Desbuches, carried a nightly greeting to the queen, with orders not to leave the Palais Royal without seeing the young sovereign. The excuse for this intrusion was, that *Monsieur* could not, without this evidence, satisfy the excited citizens that the king was safe. This was a terrible humiliation to the queen regent.

Cardinal Mazarin, having passed the night at St. Germain, commenced traveling by slow stages toward Havre. He was expecting every hour to be joined by the queen regent and other members of the royal household. He was, however, overtaken by a courier, who announced to him what had transpired in Paris, and that the escape of the royal family was impossible. The cardinal thus found himself really in exile, and earnest endeavors were made by the Fronde to induce the queen regent to secure a cardinal's hat for M. de Retz, and make him her prime minister. The last act of the queen regent was the issuing of a decree that Mazarin was banished forever from the kingdom.

Such was the posture of affairs when, on the 5th of September, 1651, the minority of the dauphin ceased. He now entered upon his fourteenth year, and, immature boy as he was, was declared to be the absolute monarch of France.

It was immediately announced to the Parliament by the grand master of ceremonies that on the seventh day of the month the king would hold his bed of justice. This name was given to the throne which the king took at extraordinary meetings of Parliament. The bed, or couch, was furnished with five cushions, and stood under a gorgeous canopy. Upon this couch the king extended himself, leaning upon the cushions.

KARTINDO PUBLISHING HOUSE (Kartindo.Com)

The ceremony was attended with all the pomp which the wealth and taste of the empire could create. As, in the morning, the court left the Palais Royal, a band of trumpeters led the van, causing the air to resound with their bugle peals. These were followed by a troop of light-horse, succeeded by two hundred of the highest nobility of France, splendidly mounted and in dazzling array. But it is vain to attempt to describe the gorgeous procession of dignitaries, mounted on tall war-horses, caparisoned with housings embroidered with silver and gold, and accompanied by numerous retainers. The attire of these attendants, from the most haughty man of arms to the humblest page, was as varied, picturesque, and glittering as human ingenuity could devise.

The young king himself rode upon a magnificent cream-colored charger. He was a beautiful boy, well formed and tall for his age. Apparently deeply impressed with the grandeur of the occasion, he appeared calm and dignified to a degree which attracted the admiration of every beholder. As he sat gracefully upon his horse, he appeared almost like a golden statue, for his dress was so elaborately embroidered with gold that neither its material or its color could be distinguished. His high-mettled charger became frightened by the shouts of "Long live the king" which burst so enthusiastically from the lips of the crowd. But Louis managed the animal with so much skill and self-possession as to increase the admiration with which all seemed to regard him. After attending mass, the young monarch took his seat in the Parliament. Here the boy of thirteen, covering his head, while all the notabilities of France stood before him with heads uncovered, repeated the following words:

"GENTLEMEN,--I have attended my Parliament in order to inform you that, according to the law of my kingdom, I shall myself assume its government. I trust that, by the goodness of God, it will be with piety and justice. My chancellor will inform you more particularly of my intentions."

The chancellor then made a long address. At its conclusion the queen mother rose and said to her son:

"SIRE,--This is the ninth year in which, by the last will of the deceased king, my much honored lord, I have been intrusted with the care of your education and the government of the state. God having by his will blessed my endeavors, and preserved your person, which is so precious to your subjects, now that the law of the kingdom calls you to the rule of this monarchy, I transfer to you, with great satisfaction, the power which had been granted me to govern. I trust that God will aid you with his strength and wisdom, that your reign may be prosperous."

KARTINDO PUBLISHING HOUSE (Kartindo.Com)

To this the king replied, "I thank you, madame, for the care which it has pleased you to take of my education and the administration of my kingdom. I pray you to continue to me your good advice, and desire that, after myself, you should be the head of my council."

The mother and the son embraced each other, and then resumed their conspicuous seats on the platform. The king's brother, Philip, duke of Anjou, next rose, and, sinking upon his knee, took the oath of allegiance to his royal brother. He was followed in this act by all the civil and ecclesiastical notabilities. The royal procession returned to the gates of the Palais Royal, greeted apparently by the unanimous acclamations of the people.

Thus a stripling, who had just completed his thirteenth year, was accepted by the nobles and by the populace as the absolute and untrammeled sovereign of France. He held in his hands, virtually unrestrained by constitution or court, their liberties, their fortunes, and their lives. It is often said that every nation has as good a government as it deserves. In republican America, it seems incredible that a nation of twenty millions of people could have been guilty of the folly of surrendering themselves to the sway of a pert, weak, immature boy of thirteen years.

The young king, in those early years, was celebrated for his gallantry. A bevy of young beauties, from the most illustrious families in the realm, crowded his court. The matter of the marriage of the king was deemed of very great moment. According to the etiquette of the times, it was thought necessary that he should marry a lady of royal blood. It would have been esteemed a degradation for him to select the daughter of the highest noble, unless that noble were of the royal family. But these pretty girls were not unconscious of the power of their charms. The haughty Anne of Austria was constantly harassed by the flirtations in which the young king was continually engaging with these lovely maidens of the court.

Louis by nature, and still more by education, was egotistical, haughty, and overbearing. His brother Philip, on the contrary, was gentle, retiring, and effeminate. The young king wished to be the handsomest man of his court, the most brilliant in wit, and the most fascinating in the graces of social life. He was very jealous of any one of his companions who might be regarded as his rival in personal beauty, or in any intellectual or courtly accomplishment. His mother encouraged this feeling. She desired that her son should stand in his court without a peer.

Still Anne of Austria, in conjunction with Cardinal Mazarin, had done what she could to check the intellectual growth of her son. Wishing to retain power as long as possible, they had manifested no disposition to withdraw young Louis from the frivolities of childhood. His education had been grossly neglected. Though entirely familiar with the routine of his devotional exercises, and all the punctilios of court etiquette, he was in mental culture and general intelligence far below ordinary school-boys of his age.

Though the king was nominally the absolute ruler of France, still there were outside influences which exerted over him a great control. There is no such thing as independent power. All are creatures of circumstances. There were two antagonistic forces brought to bear upon the young king. Anne of Austria for nine years had been regent. With the aid of her prime minister, Cardinal Mazarin, she had governed the realm. This power could not at once and entirely pass from their hands to the ignorant boy who was dallying with the little beauties in the saloons of the Palais Royal. Though Mazarin was in exile--an exile to which the queen regent had been compelled to assent--still he retained her confidence, and an influence over her mind.

On the other hand, there was the Parliament, composed mainly of proud, haughty, powerful nobles, the highest dignitaries of Church and State. This body was under the leadership of the coadjutor, M. de Retz. The antagonism between the Parliament and the court was by no means appeased. The great conflict now rose, which continued through months and years, between them, as to which should obtain the control of the king. Impelled by the action of the Parliament, the king had applied to the pope for a cardinal's hat to be conferred upon M. de Retz. This dignity attained would immeasurably increase the power of the coadjutor.

In the mean time, Cardinal Mazarin, who had fled to Spain, had re-entered France with an army of six thousand men. Paris was thrown into a state of great agitation. Parliament was immediately assembled. The king sent them a message requesting the Parliament not to regard the movements of the cardinal with any anxiety, "since the intentions of his eminence were well known by the court." This, of course, increased rather than diminished the fears of the nobles. Notwithstanding the message of the king, a decree was immediately passed declaring the cardinal and his adherents disturbers of the public peace. The cardinal was outlawed. A sum equal to thirty thousand dollars, the proceeds of the sale of some property of the cardinal, was offered to any one who should deliver him either dead or alive. Unintimidated, Mazarin continued his march toward Paris, arriving at Poictiers at the end of January, one month after having re-entered France. The king, the queen regent, and the whole court advanced there to meet him. They received him with the greatest demonstrations of joy.

When the news reached the capital that Mazarin had thus triumphantly returned, Parliament and the populace were thrown into a state of great excitement. The Duke of Orleans was roused as never before. The hostile demonstrations in Paris became so alarming, that the royal family adopted the bold resolve to return immediately to the capital. The king commenced his march at the head of the troops of the cardinal. When he reached Blois, he tarried there for a couple of days to concentrate his forces. Civil war was now inaugurated, though on rather a petty scale, between the hostile forces in various parts of the kingdom. The Prince of Condé was the prominent leader of the Parliamentary troops.

The city of Blois is situated on the right bank of the River Loire, about forty-five miles below the city of Orleans, which is also on the northern side of the same stream. At Blois, the court learned to its consternation that the Mazarin army had been attacked at Orleans by the Prince de Condé and utterly routed, with the loss of many prisoners, nearly three thousand horses, and a large part of its ordnance stores. The royal party, which was at this time in a state of great destitution, was quite overwhelmed by the disaster. The queen ordered all the equipages and baggage to be transported to the south side of the Loire, and the bridge to be broken down. At midnight, in the midst of a scene of great terror and confusion, this movement was accomplished. As the morning dawned, the carriages, crowded with the ladies of the court, were seen on the left bank of the stream, ready for flight. The queen was, for the only time in her life, so dejected as to seem utterly in despair. She feared that the triumph of the Fronde at Orleans would induce every city in the kingdom to close its gates against the court.

The royal fugitives retreated to Montereau. In the disorder of the flight they were exposed to great privation. Even the young king lost several of his best horses. Thence they proceeded to Corbeil, on the right bank of the Seine, about twelve leagues from Versailles. Here a scene occurred which is graphically described by M. Laporte, an eye-witness, who was a prominent attendant of his majesty.

"The king," writes Laporte, "insisted that *Monsieur*[E] should sleep in his room, which was so small that but one person could pass at a time. In the morning, as they lay awake, the king inadvertently spat upon the bed of *Monsieur*, who immediately spat upon the king's bed in return. Thereupon

Louis, getting angry, spat in his brother's face. When they could spit no longer, they proceeded to drag each other's sheets upon the floor, after which they prepared to fight. During this quarrel I did what I could to restrain the king. As I could not succeed, I sent for M. de Villeroi, who re-established peace. *Monsieur* lost his temper sooner than the king, but the king was much more difficult to appease."

[Footnote E: As Louis XIV. was now king, his brother Philip, eleven years of age, according to usage, took the title of *Monsieur*. The title for a time adhered still to the Duke of Orleans, brother of Louis XIII.]

It is very evident that aristocratic titles, and all the formalities of court etiquette, do not change the nature of boyhood. Though one of these little belligerents bore the title of Louis XIV., king of France, and the other was called Monsieur, the duke of Anjou, they were in character like all other ungoverned and ungovernable boys.

The court, not venturing to enter Paris, pursued its way by a circuitous route to St. Germain, leaving the city on the left. Here an additional gloom was cast over their spirits by the intelligence of very decided acts of hostility manifested against them by the inhabitants of the metropolis. The court was in a state of great embarrassment, without any money, and without possibility of obtaining stores from the capital. It was supposed that Cardinal Mazarin, noted for his selfishness, had taken good care of himself. But he declared that he was as poor as the meanest soldier in the ranks.

While at St. Germain, there was another petty conflict between the Parliamentary forces and those of the court in the vicinity of Etampes, about forty miles from Versailles. The Fronde was routed with loss. The glad tidings was brought by a courier at night to St. Germain. The news was too good to be kept till morning. M. Villeroi, to whom it was at first communicated, hastened to the chamber of the king and the Duke of Anjou, to awake them from sleep and inform them of the victory. They both, Laporte informs us, sprang from their beds, and rushed, in their slippers, night caps, and dressing-gowns, to the chamber of the cardinal, whom they awakened with the joyful tidings. He hurried in his turn with them, and in the same unsophisticated costume, to the chamber of the queen, to announce the intelligence to her.

The destitution of Louis XIV. while at St. Germain was such that he borrowed one hundred and ten francs from Moreau, one of his valets, for some replenishment of his wardrobe. Subsequently the valet, learning that the king had obtained possession of one hundred *louis d'or*, applied for payment of the debt; but the king had already expended the coin.

The routed troops of Condé took refuge within the walls of Etampes. The court, in its elation, immediately proceeded from St. Germain to the scene of conflict, to take part in the siege. This was the first serious campaign of the young king. As, attended by his suite, he examined the works, he was at one time under fire, and several bullets passed near him. Still young as he was, he had sufficient regard for his reputation and control over himself not to manifest the slightest fear.

The scenes of war which here presented themselves to the young monarch were painful in the extreme. He was every where surrounded by sick and dying soldiers. But he had no money with which to relieve their misery, and when finally the city of Etampes was taken, the spectacle of starvation, woe, and death was more awful than words can express.

As the king was entering the city, he passed a group lying upon the ground, consisting or a mother and three children, huddled closely together. The mother had died of starvation. Two of the skeleton children were also dead by her side, and the third, a babe, was straining at the exhausted breast, which could no longer afford it any nourishment.

The Prince de Condé retreated to Paris with about three thousand men. The royal troops, eight thousand in number, pursued. Each party gathered re-enforcements, so that the Prince de Condé, with about five thousand men, held at bay the royal troops, then numbering about ten thousand. The citizens, as we have mentioned, were in sympathy with the Parliament. They hated Cardinal Mazarin, and with good reason regarded the king as a prisoner in his hands. The king also detested Mazarin personally, while the force of circumstances compelled him to regard the cardinal as the advocate of the royal cause.

A very severe battle was fought between the two parties in the Faubourg St. Antoine. The ranks of the Fronde, shattered by overpowering numbers, were, in a disordered retreat, hotly pursued by their foes under Marshal Turenne. The carnage was dreadful. Suddenly the cannon of the Bastile flamed out in rapid succession, hurling their deadly shot through the compact masses of the Royalists. They recoiled and fled in confusion. Paris was in the hands of the Fronde. The populace surged through the streets, shouting "Long live the king!

Death to Mazarin!"

The cardinal, taking the king with him, retired to St. Denis. Turenne re-collected his scattered forces at Pontoise, about twenty miles north from Versailles. The cardinal, with the king, took refuge at that place in the centre of Turenne's army. Here the king issued an ordinance, transferring the Parliament from Paris to Pontoise; but the Parliament replied "that they could not obey the royal command so long as Cardinal Mazarin, whom they had outlawed, remained in France." They also issued an ordinance of their own, forbidding any member of the Parliament to leave Paris. The king, we know not under what influences, acquiesced in both of these decrees. This led the cardinal immediately to tender his resignation and retire. This important step changed the whole aspect of affairs. After the removal of the cardinal, all opposition to the court became rebellion against the king, to whom the Fronde professed entire allegiance.

[Illustration: THE TUILERIES.]

Parliament immediately issued a decree, thanking the king for banishing the cardinal, and imploring him to return to his good city of Paris. After some negotiation the king acceded to their wishes, and on the 17th of October arrived at St. Germain. Here a numerous civic guard and deputation hastened to greet him, and to conduct him to the metropolis. On the 20th he proceeded to Ruel, where he passed the night.

The king decided to enter the city at the head of his army. In order to render the scene more imposing, it was to take place at night, by the light of thousands of torches. The spectacle was such as Paris had rarely witnessed. The fickle people, ever ready to vibrate between the cry of hosanna and crucify, pealed forth their most enthusiastic rejoicings. The triumphant boy-king took possession of the Tuileries. Cardinal de Retz, who had now gained his long-coveted ecclesiastical distinction, hastened to congratulate the king and his mother upon their return to the city, from which they had so long been banished. The Duke of Orleans, chagrined and humiliated, retired to Blois.

The king soon held what was called a bed of justice, in which, instead of granting a general amnesty, he denounced the princes Condé and Conti, and other of the prominent leaders of the Fronde, as traitors to their king, to be punished by death. These doomed ones were nobles of high rank, vast wealth, with thousands of retainers. Many throughout the kingdom were in sympathy with them. They would not die without a struggle. Hence the war, which had hitherto raged between Mazarin and the Fronde, was renewed between the king and the Fronde. All over the provinces the hostile forces were rallying themselves for the conflict.

It was necessary that the Parliament should register this decree of the king. It did so, but Cardinal de Retz refused to give his vote. He very respectfully declared to the king that he, having been on friendly terms and in co-operation with the Prince de Condé, it would be neither courteous nor just for him to vote his condemnation.

This enraged both the king and his mother. They said it proved that he was in sympathy with their enemies. The court did not venture at once to strike down one so formidable. A mission was assigned the cardinal at Rome, to remove him from the country. He refused to accept it. The boy-king was growing reckless, passionate, self-willed. He began to feel the power that was in his hand. The cardinal was warned of his danger. He smiled, and said "that, sustained by his ecclesiastical rank, he had nothing to fear."

The court issued an order for the arrest of the cardinal. It was placed in the hands of Pradelle for execution. But the king was told that the cardinal would never suffer himself to be arrested without resistance; that, to secure his seizure, it might be necessary to take his life. The king seized a pen and wrote at the bottom of the order,

"I have commanded Pradelle to execute the present order on the person of De Retz, and even to arrest him, dead or alive, in the event of resistance on his part.

"LOUIS."

It was deemed very important to arrest the cardinal, if possible, without exciting a popular tumult. The palace of the cardinal was well guarded. He never went out without a numerous retinue. Should the populace of Paris see him endangered, they would spring to his rescue.

At length De Retz was earnestly invited to visit the queen at the Louvre, in token that he was not hostile to the court. It was one of the most dishonorable of stratagems. The cardinal was caught in the trap. As he was entering the antechamber of the queen upon this visit of friendship, all unsuspicious of treachery, the captain of the guard, who had been stationed there for the purpose with several gendarmes, seized him, hurried him through the great gallery of the Louvre, and down the stairs to the door. Here a royal carriage was awaiting him. He was thrust into the carriage, and five or six officers took seats by his side. To guard against any possibility of rescue, a numerous military escort was at hand. The horses were driven rapidly through the streets, and out through the Porte St. Antoine.

At nine o'clock the cardinal found himself a prisoner at the castle of Vincennes. The apartment assigned him was cold and dreary, without furniture and without a bed. Here the prisoner remained a fortnight, in the middle of December, with no fire.

The arrest of the cardinal created a great sensation throughout Paris. But the chateau was too strong, and too vigilantly guarded by the royal troops, to encourage any attempt at a rescue.

[Illustration: THE CASTLE OF VINCENNES.]

In the mean time, Mazarin had placed himself at the head of the royal troops in one of the provinces, where he gained several unimportant victories over the bands of the Fronde. These successes were trumpeted abroad as great achievements, so as to invest the cardinal with the renown of a great conqueror. Mazarin was well aware of the influence of military glory upon the populace in Paris. The king also began to feel the need of his dominant mind. He was invited to return to Paris. Louis himself rode out six miles beyond the walls to receive him. The cardinal entered the city in triumph, in the same carriage with his sovereign, and seated by his side. All the old idols were forgotten, and the once detested Mazarin was received as though he were an angel from heaven. Bonfires and illuminations blazed through the streets; the whole city resounded with demonstrations of rejoicing. Thus terminated the year 1652.

The first care of Cardinal Mazarin, after his return to Paris, was to restore the finances, which were in a deplorable condition. Louis was fond of pleasure. It was one great object of the cardinal to gratify him in this respect, in every possible way. Notwithstanding the penury of the court, the cardinal contrived to supply the king with money. Thus, during the winter, the royal palaces resounded with festivity and dissipation. The young king became very fond of private theatricals, in which he, his brother Philip, and the young ladies of the court took prominent parts. Louis often appeared upon the stage in the character of a ballet-dancer. He was proud of the grace with which he could perform the most difficult pirouettes. He had plays written, with parts expressly composed for his aristocratic troop.

The scene of these masqueradings was the theatre of the Hotel du Petit Bourbon, which was contiguous to the Louvre. When royalty plays and courtiers fill pit and gallery, applause is without stint. The boy-king was much elated with his theatric triumphs. The queen and Cardinal Mazarin were well pleased to see the king expending his energies in that direction.

These entertainments cost money, which Mazarin was greatly embarrassed in obtaining. The hour was approaching for the coronation of Louis. The pageant would require large sums of money to invest the occasion with the desirable splendor. But gold was not all that was wanted. Rank, brilliance, beauty were requisite suitably to impress the masses of the people. But the civil war had robbed the court of many of its most attractive ornaments.

Monsieur, the duke of Orleans, was sullenly residing at Blois. Here he held a somewhat rival court to the king. He refused to attend the coronation unless certain concessions were granted, to which Mazarin could not give his consent. Mademoiselle, the duchess of Montpensier, daughter of Monsieur by his first wife, a young lady of wonderful heroism and attractions, who possessed an enormous property in her own right, and who was surrounded by a brilliant court of her own, could not consistently share in festivities at which her father refused to appear.

The Prince of Condé, one of the highest nobles of the realm, and who had many adherents of the most illustrious rank, was in arms against his king at the head of the Spanish forces, and sentence of death had been pronounced upon him.

Cardinal de Retz was a prisoner at Vincennes. His numerous followers in Church and State refused to sanction by their presence any movements of a court thus persecuting their beloved cardinal.

It was thus impossible to invest the coronation with the splendor which the occasion seemed to demand.

The coronation took place, however, at Rheims. Cardinal Mazarin exerted all his ingenuity to render the pageant imposing; but the absence of so many of the most illustrious of the realm cast an atmosphere of gloom around the ceremonies.

France was at the time at war with Spain. The Fronde co-operated with the Spanish troops in the civil war. Immediately after the coronation, the king, then sixteen years of age, left Rheims to place himself at the head of the army. He repaired to Stenay, on the Meuse, in the extreme northeastern frontier of France. This ancient city, protected by strong fortifications, was held by Condé. The royal troops were besieging it. The poverty of the treasury was such that Mazarin could not furnish Louis even with the luxury of a carriage. He traveled on horseback. He had no table of his own, but shared in that of the Marquis de Fabert, the general in command.

It seems difficult to account for the fact that the young king was permitted to enter the trenches, and to engage in skirmishes, where he was so exposed to the fire of the enemy that the wounded and the dead were continually falling around him. He displayed much courage on these occasions.

The Prince of Condé left a garrison in one of the strong fortresses, and marched with the main body of his troops to Arras. The movements of the two petty armies, their skirmishes and battles, are no longer of any interest. The battles were fought and the victories gained by the direction of the generals Turenne and Fabert. Though the boy-king displayed intrepidity which secured for him the respect of the soldiers, he could exert but little influence either in council or on the field. Both Stenay and Arras were soon taken. The army of the Prince of Condé was driven from all its positions.

The king returned to Paris to enjoy the gratulation of the populace, and to offer public thanksgiving in the cathedral of Notre Dame.

KARTINDO PUBLISHING HOUSE (Kartindo.Com)

CHAPTER III

MATRIMONIAL PROJECTS

1653-1656

Gayeties in Paris.--Poverty of the court.--Death of the Archbishop of Paris.--Murmurings.--Escape of Cardinal de Retz.--Manoeuvres of Anne of Austria.--Olympia de Mancini.--Henrietta of England.--Embarrassment of Henrietta.--Rudeness of Louis XIV.--Royal quarrel.--Independence of the king.--Order of the king.--Audacity of Louis.--Submission of Parliament.--A tournament.--Christina of Sweden.--Reception of Christina.--Her eccentric character.--Astonishment of Anne of Austria.--Varied information of Christina.--Rudeness of the ex-queen.--She visits Mademoiselle.--Christina returns to Sweden.--Outbreak of Christina.--Letter to Cardinal Mazarin.--Count de Soissons.--Marriage of Olympia Mancini.--Mademoiselle d'Argencourt.--The Pope's choir.--Mary Mancini.--Description of Mary Mancini.--Mary Mancini becomes a member of the court.--Her influence over Louis.--Ambitious views of Mazarin.--Projects for the marriage of Louis XIV.--Diplomatic efforts with Spain.--The Princess of Orange.--Power of Mary Mancini.--The Princess Marguerite.--Anger of the queen regent.--Decision of the cabinet.--New negotiations.--The two courts arrange to meet at Lyons.--Fickleness of Louis.--The royal parties meet.--The Princess Marguerite.--Sorrows of Mary.

"There is nothing so successful as success." The young king returned to Paris from his coronation and his brief campaign a hero and a conqueror. The courage he had displayed won universal admiration. The excitable populace were half frenzied with enthusiasm. The city resounded with shouts of gladness, and the streets were resplendent with the display of gorgeous pageants.

The few nobles who still rallied around the court endeavored to compensate by the magnificence of their equipages, the elegance of their attire, and the splendor of their festivities, for their diminished numbers. There were balls and tournaments, where the dress and customs of the by-gone ages of chivalry were revived. Ladies of illustrious birth, glittering in jewels, and proud in conscious beauty, contributed to the gorgeousness of the spectacle. Still, in the midst of all this splendor, the impoverished court was greatly embarrassed by straitened circumstances.

Cardinal Mazarin, eager to retain his hold upon the king, did everything he could to gratify the love of pleasure which his royal master developed, and strove to multiply seductive amusements to engross his time and thoughts.

But a few days after Cardinal de Retz had been conducted a prisoner to Vincennes, his uncle, the Archbishop of Paris, died. The cardinal could legally claim the succession. The metropolitan clergy, who had been almost roused to rebellion by his arrest, were now still more deeply moved, since he had become their archbishop. They regarded his captivity as political martyrdom, and their murmurs were deep and prolonged. The pope also addressed several letters to the court, soliciting the liberation of his cardinal. The excitement daily increased. Nearly all the pulpits more or less openly denounced his captivity. At length a pamphlet appeared urging the clergy to close all their churches till their archbishop should be released.

Mazarin was frightened. He sent an envoy to the captive cardinal presenting terms of compromise. We have not space to describe the diplomacy which ensued, but the conference was unavailing. The cardinal was soon after removed, under an escort of dragoons, to the fortress of Nantes. From this place he almost miraculously escaped to his own territory of Retz, where he was regarded as sovereign, and where he was surrounded by retainers who, in impregnable castles, would fight to the death for their lord. These scenes took place early in the summer of 1653.

In the mean time, the young king was amusing himself in his various palaces with the many beautiful young ladies who embellished his court. Like other lads of fifteen, he was in the habit of falling in love with one and another, though the transient passion did not seem very deeply to affect his heart. Some of these maidens were exceedingly beautiful. In others, vivacity and intellectual brilliance quite eclipsed the charms of the highest physical loveliness.

Anne of Austria, forgetting that the all-dominant passion of love had led her to regret that she was the wife of the king, that she might marry the Duke of Buckingham, did not deem it possible that her son could stoop so low as to marry any one who was not of royal blood. She therefore regarded without much uneasiness his desperate flirtations, while she was scanning the courts of Europe in search of an alliance which would add to the power and the renown of her son.

One of the nieces of Cardinal Mazarin, an Italian girl by the name of Olympia Mancini, was among the first to whom the boy-king of fifteen became specially attached. Olympia was very beautiful, and her personal fascinations were rivaled by her mental brilliance, wit, and tact. She was by nature and education a thorough coquette, amiable and endearing to an unusual degree. She had a sister a little older than herself, who was also extremely beautiful, who had recently become the Duchess of Mercoeur. Etiquette required that in the balls which the king attended every evening he should recognize the rank of the duchess by leading her out first in the dance. After this, he devoted himself exclusively, for the remainder of the evening, to Olympia.

It will be remembered that Henrietta, the widowed queen of Charles II., who was daughter of Henry IV. and sister of Louis XIII., was then residing in France. She had no pecuniary means of her own, and, chagrined and humiliated, was a pensioner upon the bounty of the impoverished French court. Henrietta had with her a very pretty daughter, eleven years of age. Being the granddaughter of Henry IV. and daughter of Charles II., she was entitled, through the purity of her royal blood, to the highest consideration in the etiquette of the court. But the mother and the daughter, from their poverty and their misfortunes, were precluded from any general participation in the festivities of the palace.

The queen, Anne of Austria, on one occasion, gave a private ball in honor of these unfortunate guests in her own apartments. None were invited but a few of her most intimate friends. Henrietta attended with her daughter, who bore her mother's name. There are few situations more painful than that of poor relatives visiting their more prosperous friends, who in charity condescend to pay them some little attention. The young Henrietta was a fragile and timid girl, who keenly felt the embarrassment of her situation. As, with her face suffused with blushes, and her eyes moistened with the conflicting emotions of joyousness and fear, she entered the brilliant saloon of Anne of Austria, crowded with those below her in rank, but above her in prosperity and all worldly aggrandizement, she was received coldly, with no marks of sympathy or attention. As the music summoned the dancers to the floor, the king, neglecting his young and royal cousin, advanced, according to his custom, to the Duchess of Mercoeur, to lead her out. The queen, shocked at so gross a breach of etiquette, and even of kindly feeling, rose from her seat, and, advancing, withdrew the hand of the duchess from her son, and said to him, in a low voice, "You should dance first with the English princess." The boy-king sulkily replied, "I am not fond of little girls." Both Henrietta and her daughter overheard this uncourteous and cruel remark.

KARTINDO PUBLISHING HOUSE (Kartindo.Com)

Henrietta, the mother, hastened to the queen, and entreated her not to attempt to constrain the wishes of his majesty. It was an exceedingly awkward position for all the parties. The spirit of Anne of Austria was aroused. Resuming her maternal authority, she declared that if her niece, the Princess of England, were to remain a spectator at the ball, her son should do the same. Thus constrained, Louis very ungraciously led out Henrietta upon the floor. The young princess, tender in years, sensitive through sorrow, wounded and heart-crushed, danced with tears streaming down her cheeks.

Upon the departure of the guests, the mother and the son had their first serious quarrel. Anne rebuked Louis severely for his shameful conduct. The king rebelled. Haughtily facing his mother, he said, "I have long enough been guided by your leading-strings. I shall submit to it no longer." It was a final declaration of independence. Though there were tears shed on both sides, and the queen made strenuous efforts at conciliation, she felt, and justly felt, that the control of her son had passed from her forever. It was a crisis in the life of the king. From that hour he seemed disposed on all occasions to assert his manhood.

A remarkable indication of this soon occurred. It was customary, when the king, through his ministers, issued any decrees, that they should be registered by the Parliament, to give them full authority. Some very oppressive decrees had been issued to raise funds for the court. It was deemed very important that they should be registered. The king in person attended Parliament, that the influence of his presence might carry the measure. No one dared to oppose in the presence of the king.

Louis had now established his summer residence at the castle of Vincennes. Arrangements had been made for a magnificent hunt in the forest the next day, to be attended by all the ladies and gentlemen of the court. The king, after leaving the Parliament, returned to Vincennes, which is about three miles from Paris. He had scarcely arrived at the castle when he received information that, immediately upon his leaving the Parliament, a motion had been made to reconsider the approval of the decrees.

The king dispatched a courier ordering the Chamber to reassemble the next morning. The pleasure-loving courtiers were dismayed by this order, as they thought it would interfere with the hunt. But the king assured them that business should not be allowed to interfere with his pleasures.

At half past nine o'clock the next morning the king entered the chamber of deputies in his hunting-dress. It consisted of a scarlet coat, a gray beaver hat, and high military boots. He was followed by a large retinue of the nobles of his court in a similar costume.

"In this unusual attire," writes the Marquis de Montglat, "the king heard mass, took his place with the accustomed ceremonies, and, with a whip in his hand, declared to the Parliament that in future it was his will that his edicts should be registered, and not discussed. He threatened them that, should the contrary occur, he would return and enforce obedience."

How potent must have been the circumstances which the feudalism of ages had created. These assembled nobles yielded without a murmur to this insolence from a boy of eighteen. Parliament had ventured to try its strength against Cardinal Mazarin, but did not dare to disobey its king.

Soon after this, Louis, having learned that Turenne had gained some important victories over the Fronde, decided to join the army to witness the siege of the city of Condé and of St. Quilain. Both of these places soon fell into the hands of the Royalist troops. The king had looked on. Rapidly he returned to Paris to enjoy almost a Roman triumph for his great achievement.

As one of the festivities of the city, the king arranged a tournament in honor of his avowed lady-love, Olympia Mancini. She occupied a conspicuous seat among the ladies of the court, her lovely person decorated with a dress of exquisite taste and beauty. The king was prominent in his attire among all the knights assembled to contest the palm of chivalry. He was dressed in robes of brilliant scarlet. A white scarf encircled his waist, and snow-white plumes waved gracefully from his hat.

The scene was as gorgeous as the wealth and decorative art of the court could create. There were retainers surrounding the high lords, and heralds, and pages, and trumpeters, all arrayed in the most picturesque costume. No one could be so discourteous or impolitic as to vanquish the king. He consequently bore away all the laurels. This magnificent tournament gave the name of "The Carousal" to the space where it was held, between the Louvre and the Tuileries.

Early in the summer the court removed to Compiègne, to spend the season in rural amusements there. Christina, the young queen of Sweden, who had just abdicated the throne, and whose eccentricities had attracted the attention of Europe, came to the frontiers of France with an imposing retinue, and,

KARTINDO PUBLISHING HOUSE (Kartindo.Com)

announcing her arrival, awaited the invitation of the king to visit his court. She was one of the most extraordinary personages of that or any age. Good looking, "strong minded" to the highest degree, masculine in dress and address, always self-possessed, absolutely fearing nothing, proud, haughty, speaking fluently eight languages, familiar with art, and a consummate *intriguante*, she excited astonishment and a certain degree of admiration wherever she appeared.

The curiosity of Louis was so greatly excited and so freely expressed to see this extraordinary personage as to arouse the jealousy of Olympia. The king perceived this. It is one of the most detestable traits in our fallen nature that one can take pleasure in making another unhappy. The unamiable king amused himself in torturing the feelings of Olympia.

[Illustration: PALACE OF CHANTILLY.]

Christina proceeded at first to Paris. Here she was received with the greatest honor. For a distance of nearly six miles from the Louvre the streets were lined with armed citizens, who greeted her with almost unintermitted applause. The crowd was so great that, though she reached the suburbs of Paris at two o'clock in the afternoon, she did not alight at the Louvre until nine o'clock in the evening. This eccentric princess was then thirty years of age, and, though youthful in appearance, in dress and manners she affected the Amazon. She had great powers of pleasing, and her wit, her entire self-reliance, and extensive information, enabled her to render herself very attractive whenever she wished to do so.

After spending a few days in Paris, she proceeded to Compiègne to visit the king and queen. Louis and his brother, with Mazarin and a crowd of courtiers, rode out as far as Chantilly, a distance of nearly twenty miles, to meet her. Christina also traveled in state, accompanied by an imposing retinue. Here there was, at that time, one of the largest and finest structures in France. The castle belonged to the family of Condé. The opposite cut presents it to the reader as it then appeared.

The king and his brother, from some freak, presented themselves to her at first *incognito*. They were introduced by Mazarin as two of the most nobly born gentlemen in France. Christina smiled, and promptly replied,

"Yes, I have no doubt of it, since their birthright is a crown."

She had seen their portraits in the Louvre the day before, and immediately recognized them.

Christina was to be honored with quite a triumphal entrance to Compiègne. The king accordingly returned to Compiègne, and the next day, with the whole court in carriages, rode out a few leagues to a very splendid mansion belonging to one of the nobles at Fayet. It was a lovely day, warm and cloudless. Anne of Austria decided to receive her illustrious guest upon the spacious terrace. There she assembled her numerous court, resplendent with gorgeous dresses, and blazing with diamonds. Soon the carriage of the Swedish queen drove up, with the loud clatter of outriders and the flourish of trumpets. Cardinal Mazarin and the Duke de Guise assisted her to alight. As she ascended the terrace the queen advanced to meet her.

Though Anne was at first struck with amazement at the ludicrous appearance of the attire of Christina, she was immediately fascinated by her conversational tact and brilliance. Some allusion having been made to the portrait of the king in the Louvre, the queen held out her arm to show a still more faithful miniature in the clasp of her bracelet. Anne of Austria had a very beautiful arm, and was very proud of it. Christina, instead of looking at the bracelet, surveyed the undraped arm and hand with admiration.

"How beautiful! how beautiful!" she exclaimed. "Never did I see an arm and hand of such lovely hue and such exquisite symmetry. I would willingly have made the journey from Rome to Paris to see this arm."

The queen's heart was won, Christina knew it. The next achievement was to win the king.

Christina was apparently as familiar with the French court, and all the intrigues there, from the information which she had obtained, as if she had always been a resident at that court. She immediately turned with very marked attention to Olympia Mancini, and seemed dazzled by her beauty. The heart of the boy-king was won in seeing his own good taste thus highly appreciated and sanctioned. Having thus secured the queen and the king, Christina was well aware that she had captivated the whole court.

An elegant collation was prepared. The plump little queen ate like a hungry dragoon. The royal cortège, enveloping the Swedish princess, returned to the palace of Compiègne. Several days were spent at Compiègne, during which she astonished every one by the remarkable self-poise of her character, her varied information, and the versatility of her talents. She conversed upon theology with the ecclesiastics, upon politics with the ministers, upon all branches of science and art with philosophers and the *virtuosi*, and eclipsed the most brilliant of the courtiers in the small-talk of gallantry.

She attended the theatre with the queen. During the tragedy she wept like a child, heartily and unaffectedly. During the farce, which was one of those coarse and pungent compositions by the poet Scarron, which would now be scarcely tolerated, her shouts of laughter echoed through the theatre. She astonished the court by clapping her hands and throwing her feet upon the top of the royal box, like a rowdy in a smoking-room.

[Illustration: VIEW OF FONTAINEBLEAU.]

From Compiègne, Christina, by invitation, went to Fontainebleau to visit Mademoiselle de Montpensier. The piquant pen of Mademoiselle has described this interview. Some allowance must perhaps be made for the vein of satire which pervaded nearly all the utterances of this haughty princess. The dress of Christina consisted of a skirt of gray silk, trimmed with gold and silver lace, with a bodice of gold-colored camlet trimmed like the skirt. She wore a kerchief of Genoa point about her neck, fastened with a knot of white ribbon. A light wig concealed her natural hair. Her hat was profusely decorated with white plumes. She looked, upon the whole, Mademoiselle thought, like a handsome boy.

Mademoiselle, accustomed to the rigid propriety of the French court, was not a little surprised to hear Christina, during the comedy, interlard her conversation with hearty oaths, with all the volubility of an old guardsman. She flung about her legs in the most astonishing manner, throwing them over the arms of her chair, and placing herself in attitudes quite unprecedented in Parisian circles.

Soon after this, this Amazonian princess returned by a circuitous route to her Northern home. Before taking leave of her, it may be well to remark that subsequently Christina made a second visit to France uninvited--not only uninvited, but very unwelcome. She took possession of the palace of Fontainebleau with her attendants, where with cold courtesy she was tolerated. In a freak of passion, she accused her grand equerry, M. Monaldeschi, of high treason, and actually put him to death. So high-handed an outrage, even in those days of feudal barbarism, excited throughout France a universal feeling of

KARTINDO PUBLISHING HOUSE (Kartindo.Com)

disgust and indignation. The sentiment was so strong and general that the king deemed it necessary to send her a letter through his minister, Mazarin, expressive of his extreme displeasure.

Christina, much exasperated, sent a reply containing the following expressions:

"MR. MAZARIN,--Those who acquainted you with the details regarding Monaldeschi, my equerry, were very ill informed. Your proceeding ought not, however, to astonish me, silly as it is. But I should never have believed that either you or your haughty young master would have dared to exhibit the least resentment toward me. Learn all of you, valets and masters, little and great, that it was my pleasure to act as I did; that I need not, and I will not account for my actions to any one in the world, and particularly to bullies of your description. I wish you to know, and to say to all who will hear it, that Christina cares very little about your court, and still less about yourself; and that, in order to revenge my wrongs, I do not require to have recourse to your formidable power. Believe me, therefore, Jules,[F] you had better conduct yourself in a manner to deserve my favor, which you can not study too much to secure. God preserve you from ever risking the least indiscreet remark upon my person. Although at the end of the earth, I shall be informed of your plots. I have friends and courtiers in my service who are as clever and far-sighted as yours, although they are not so well paid.

"CHRISTINA."

[Footnote F: Jules, the Christian name of Mazarin.]

Soon after this her Swedish majesty disappeared from France, to the great relief of the court, and was seen there no more.

Olympia Mancini had ever increasing evidence that the love of the king for her was but a frivolous and heartless passion. The Count de Soissons, of Savoy, a young prince who had just become the head of his house, visited the court of Louis XIV. The marvelous beauty of Olympia, at first glance, won his heart. He was young, handsome, chivalric, high-born, and was just entering upon a magnificent inheritance. Olympia had recently lost by death a mother whom she greatly revered, and a beloved sister. She was overwhelmed with grief. The entire want of sympathy manifested by the king shocked her. He thought of nothing but his own personal pleasure. Regardless of the grief of Olympia, he exhibited himself, evening after evening, in court theatricals, emulating the agility of an opera-dancer, and attired in spangled robes.

Wounded and irritated by such conduct, Olympia accepted the proffered hand of the Count de Soissons, who was grandson of Charles V. The marriage was attended with great splendor at the palace of the Louvre. All the court was present. The king himself seemed not at all discomposed that another should marry the beautiful maiden whom he had professed so ardently to love. Indeed, he was already beginning to transfer his attentions to Mademoiselle d'Argencourt, a queenly beauty of the high family of Conti. Her figure was perfect, her manners were courtly in the highest degree, and all who approached her were charmed with her conversational vivacity and tact.

But Mademoiselle's affections were already engaged, and, being fully aware that the king flitted from beauty to beauty, like the butterfly from flower to flower, she very frankly intimated to the king that she could not receive his attentions. Louis was heart-broken; for such fragile hearts are easily broken and as easily repaired. He hastened to his mother, and told her that he must leave Paris to conquer his passion. The love-sick monarch retired to Vincennes, spent ten days there, and returned quite cured.

The marriage of Olympia, as we have mentioned, was celebrated with very great brilliance. The ambitious cardinal, in heart disappointed that he had not been able to confer the hand of Olympia on the king, was increasingly desirous of investing the members of his family with all possible éclat. He had imported for the occasion the principal members of the Pope's choir. These wonderful vocalists from the Sistine Chapel astonished the French court with melody and harmony such as had never been heard in the Louvre before.

Olympia had a younger sister, Mary, fifteen years of age. She had come from her school in a convent to witness the marriage festivities. The music and the impressive scene affected the artless child deeply, and her tears flowed freely. The king, surrounded by the brilliant beauties of his court, accidentally caught sight of this child. Though not beautiful, there was something in her unaffected attitude, her tears, her entire absorption in the scene, which arrested his attention.

Mary had early developed so bold, independent, and self-reliant a spirit as to induce her father, on his death-bed, to entreat Madame de Mancini to compel her to take the veil. In compliance with this injunction, Mary had been placed in a convent until she should attain the fitting age to assume the irrevocable

KARTINDO PUBLISHING HOUSE (Kartindo.Com)

vows. Thus trained in seclusion, and with no ambitious aspirations, she had acquired a character of perfect simplicity, and her countenance bore an expression of intelligence and sensibility far more attractive than ordinary beauty. A contemporaneous writer says,

"Her movements, her manners, and all the bearing of her person were the result of a nature guided by grace. Her look was tender, the accents of her voice were enchanting. Her genius was great, substantial, and extensive, and capable of the grandest conceptions. She wrote both good prose and pleasing poetry; and Mary Mancini, who shone in a courtly letter, was equally capable of producing a political or state dispatch. She would not have been unworthy of the throne if among us great merit had been entitled to obtain it."

The king inquired her name. Upon learning that she was a niece of the cardinal, and a sister of Olympia, he desired that she might be presented to him.

Mary was an enthusiast. The young king was very handsome, very courtly, and a perfect master of all the phrases of gallantry. Mary fell in love with him, without knowing it, at first sight. It was not the *monarch* which had won her, but the *man*, of exquisitely symmetrical proportions, so princely in his bearing, so fascinating in his address. The young schoolgirl returned to her convent with the image of the king indelibly engraven on her heart. The few words which passed between them interested the king, for every word she said bore the impress of her genius. Ere long she was added to the ladies of the queen's household.

The king, having closed his flirtation with Mademoiselle d'Argencourt, found himself almost insensibly drawn to Mary Mancini. Though there were many in his court more beautiful in person, there were none who could rival her in intellect and wit. Though naturally timid, her reserve disappeared when in his presence. Though ever approaching him with the utmost possible deference and respect, she conversed with him with a frankness to which he was entirely unaccustomed, and which, at the same time, surprised and charmed him.

His vanity was gratified with the almost religious devotion with which she unaffectedly regarded her sovereign, while at the same time she addressed him with a bold simplicity of utterance which astounded the courtiers and enthralled the king. He was amazed and bewildered by the grandeur of a character such as he had never encountered before. She reproved him for his faults, instructed him in his ignorance, conversed with him upon themes beyond the ordinary range of his intellect, and endeavored to enkindle within him noble impulses and a lofty ambition. The king found himself quite unable to compete with her strength of intellect. His weaker nature became more and more subject to one endowed with gifts far superior to his own. In every hour of perplexity, in every serious moment, when the better nature of the king gained a transient ascendency, he turned from the frivolity of the gay and thoughtless beings fluttering around him to Mary Mancini for guidance and strength.

The ambition of Cardinal Mazarin was again excited with the hope that he might yet place a niece upon the throne of France. But there was no end to the intrigues of ambitious aspirants, directly or indirectly, for the hand of the young king. Mademoiselle de Montpensier had enormous wealth, was of high birth, and was endowed with marvelous force of character. She had long aspired to share the throne with her young cousin. When it was evident that this plan had failed, the Duke of Orleans brought forward a younger daughter by a second wife. But Mazarin succeeded in thwarting this arrangement. The Princess Henrietta of England, whom the young king had treated so cruelly at the ball, was urged upon him. She was lovely in person, amiable in character, but in poverty and exile. Cromwell was in the plenitude of his power. There was no probability that her family would be restored to the throne. The king turned coldly from her.

Portugal was then one of the most wealthy and powerful courts of Europe. The Queen of Portugal was exceedingly anxious to unite her daughter with the King of France. Through her embassadors she endeavored to effect an alliance. A portrait of the princess was sent to Louis. It was very beautiful. The king made private inquiries. She was very plain. This settled the question. The Portuguese princess was thought of no more.

The King of Spain had a very beautiful daughter, Maria Theresa. The Spanish monarchy then, perhaps, stood second to none other on the globe. Spain and France were engaged in petty and vexatious hostilities. A matrimonial alliance would secure friendship. The matter was much talked of. The proud queen-mother, Anne of Austria, was very solicitous to secure that alliance, as it would gratify her highest ambition. Mazarin professed warmly to favor it. He probably saw insuperable obstacles in the way, but hoped, by co-operating cordially with the wishes of the queen, to be able finally to secure the marriage of the king with Mary Mancini.

Maria Theresa was heiress to the throne of Spain. Should she marry Louis XIV., it would be necessary for her to leave Spain and reside in Paris. Thus the

Queen of France would be the Queen of Spain. In fact, Spain would be annexed to France as a sort of tributary nation, the court being at Paris, and all the offices being at the disposal of the Queen of France, residing there. The pride of the Spaniards revolted from this, and still the diplomatists were conferring upon the matter.

Henrietta, the unfortunate widow of Charles I. of England, had an elder daughter, who had married the Prince of Orange, the head of the illustrious house of Nassau. This Princess of Orange was very beautiful, young, in the enjoyment of vast possessions, and a widow. She aspired to the hand, and to share the crown of the King of France. Surrounded by great magnificence and blazing with jewels, she visited the court of Louis XIV. Her mission was signally unsuccessful. The king took a strong dislike to her, and repelled her advances with marked discourtesy.

While matters were in this state, Charles II. offered his hand to Mary Mancini. But the proud cardinal would not allow his niece to marry a crownless and impoverished king. In the mean time, Mary Mancini, by her increasing beauty and her mental superiority, was gaining daily more influence over the mind of the king. With a voice of singular melody, a brilliant eye, a figure as graceful and elastic as that of a fairy, and with words of wonderful wisdom flowing, as it were, instinctively from her lips, she seemed effectually and almost unconsciously to have enthralled the king. All his previous passions were boyish and ephemeral. But Mary was very different from any other lady of the court. Her depth of feeling, her pensive yet cheerful temperament, and her full-souled sympathy in all that was truly noble in conduct and character, astonished and engrossed the susceptible monarch.

The Duchess of Savoy had a daughter, Marguerite, whom she wished to have become the wife of the French king. The princess was by birth of the highest rank, being a descendant of Henry IV. The duchess sent as an envoy a young Piedmontese count to treat secretly with the cardinal for the marriage of the king with the Princess Marguerite. The count was unsuccessful. It was quite evident that Mazarin was intending to secure the marriage of the king with his niece.

The proud queen, Anne of Austria, became greatly alarmed. She mortally offended the cardinal by declaring to him that nothing should induce her to consent to such a degradation of her son as to permit his marriage with the niece of the cardinal. She declared that in such an event she herself would head an insurrection against the king, and that the whole of France would revolt both against him and his minister. These bitter words ever after rankled in the bosom of the cardinal.

The queen summoned a secret assembly of the cabinet, and put to them the question whether the marriage of her son without her consent would be a valid one. The unanimous decision was in the negative. She then had this decision carefully drawn up, and made effectual arrangements to have it registered by the Parliament, should the king secretly marry Mary Mancini.

The cardinal now found himself compelled to abandon his ambitious hopes for his niece, and opened again negotiations with Spain for the hand of the Infanta Maria Theresa, and with the court of Savoy for the Princess Marguerite. The Spanish marriage would terminate the war. The union with Savoy would invest France with new powers for its vigorous prosecution.

Every day the attachment of the king to Mary Mancini became more undisguised. She guided his reading; she taught him the Italian language; she introduced to him the names of great men in the works of literature and art, and labored heroically to elevate his tastes, and to inspire him with the ambition of performing glorious deeds.

The queen, in her anxiety, made arrangements for the king to meet the Princess Marguerite at Lyons, that they might be betrothed. She greatly preferred the alliance with Spain; but as there seemed to be insuperable objections to that, she turned her attention to Savoy. The king continued his marked and almost exclusive attentions to Mary, and she loved him with the full flow of her ardent affections.

The whole court was to proceed in great magnificence to Lyons, to meet the court of Savoy. Mary was compelled to accompany the court. She knew full well the errand upon which Louis was bound. Though her heart was heavy, and tears dimmed her eyes, she was obliged to appear cheerful. She had made an earnest effort to avoid the journey, but Anne of Austria was obdurate and cruel. She assured Mary that she could not spare her presence when she wished to impress the Princess Marguerite with the magnificence and beauty of the French court.

The court of Savoy left Turin at the same time that the French court left Paris. The pledge had been given that, should the king be pleased with the appearance of Marguerite, the marriage should take place without delay. During the

KARTINDO PUBLISHING HOUSE (Kartindo.Com)

journey, the heartless and fickle king, ever charmed by novelty, was in buoyant spirits. Though he still clung to the side of Mary, giving her a seat in his own carriage, and, when the weather was fine, riding by her side on horseback, he tortured her heart by the joyousness with which he spoke of the anticipated charms of Marguerite and of his approaching marriage.

At Lyons the royal party was received with great magnificence. The next day it was announced that the court of Savoy was approaching. The queen-mother and her son, with two ladies in the royal coach, preceded, and, followed by a considerable retinue, advanced to meet their guests. The king mounted his horse and galloped forward to get a sight of Marguerite without being known by her. She was riding in an open barouche. He soon returned in great glee, and, springing from the saddle, re-entered the carriage, and informed his mother that the Princess Marguerite was very beautiful. Scarcely had he said this ere the two royal coaches met. Both parties alighted. The princess was introduced to Louis. Then the queen-mother and her son, the Duchess of Savoy and the Princess Marguerite, and an elder daughter, who was a widow, entered the royal coach and returned to Lyons. The king was in exuberant spirits. He at once entered into the most animated and familiar conversation with the princess.

The Princess Marguerite fully appreciated the embarrassment of her own situation. She was going to Lyons to present herself to Louis XIV. to see if he would take her for his wife. The humiliation of being rejected would be dreadful. In vain she implored her mother to spare her from such a possibility. But the question seemed to be at once settled favorably. The king was manifestly much pleased with Marguerite, and the princess could see nothing but attractions in the young, handsome, and courtly sovereign of France.

Poor Mary, who was informed of every thing that transpired, was suffering martyrdom. She was immediately forsaken and forgotten. In public, all her force of character was called into requisition to dress her face in smiles. In her secret apartment she wept bitterly.

KARTINDO PUBLISHING HOUSE (Kartindo.Com)

CHAPTER IV

THE MARRIAGE OF THE KING

1658-1661

Marguerite of Savoy.--Sudden change of prospects.--An heir to the Spanish throne.--Rejection of Marguerite.--Mazarin communicates with the Duchess of Savoy.--Private interview of Mazarin and the Duchess of Savoy.--Conduct of the king.--Movements of Mazarin.--Power of the cardinal.--Mary exiled from the court.--Mary's parting with the king.--The Isle of Pheasants.--Interview of Louis with Mary.--Negotiations with Spain.--Marriage preparations according to Spanish etiquette.--Appearance of the Infanta.--Interview of Anne of Austria and her brother.--Meeting of Louis XIV. and his bride.--Tedious ceremonies.-- Gorgeous entrance into the capital.--Cruelty of the queen-mother.--The Prince Colonna.--Mary is presented to the young Queen of France.--Misery of Mary Mancini.--Mary concludes to accept the hand of Prince Colonna.--Marriage of Mary Mancini.--Character of Louis XIV. and Maria Theresa.--Magnificent ceremonies.--Festivities continued.--Revolting state of society.--Mazarin guilty of great extortion.--Fatal accident.--Sufferings of the cardinal.--Oppressive measures of the cardinal.--Confession of Mazarin.--Advice of M. Colbert.-- Suspense of the cardinal.--His property restored.--Death of Mazarin.--His immense wealth.--Legacies of Mazarin.--Views of Louis XIV.

The Princess Marguerite of Savoy was very beautiful. She was a brunette, with large, lustrous eyes, fairy-like proportions, queenly bearing, and so graceful in every movement that she scarcely seemed to touch the ground as she walked. Her reception by the king, the queen, and the whole court was every thing that could be desired. The duchess and her daughter that night placed their heads upon their pillows with the undoubting conviction that Marguerite was to be the Queen of France. The king ordered his suite to be ready, in their gala dresses, to attend him on the morrow to the apartments of the princess.

The morning came. To the surprise and bewilderment of the court, every thing was changed. The king was thoughtful, distant, reserved. With great formality of etiquette, he called upon the princess. His countenance and manner indicated an entire change of feeling. With the coldest phrases of court etiquette he addressed her. He was civil, and civil only. The warmth of the lover had disappeared entirely. The Duchess of Savoy was astounded. Even the French court seemed stupefied by so unexpected and decisive an alteration in the aspect of affairs.

The explanation which gradually came to light was very simple. During the night a courier had arrived, in breathless haste, with the announcement that the Queen of Spain had given birth to a son. Maria Theresa was no longer heir to the throne. The way was consequently open to the Spanish marriage. This alliance would secure peace with Spain, and was altogether a more powerful and wealthy connection than that with the court of Savoy. The cardinal immediately communicated the intelligence to the queen-mother and the king. They alone knew it. Marguerite was to be rejected, and the hand of Maria Theresa to be claimed.

Mary Mancini was utterly bewildered by the change, so inexplicable to her, in the posture of affairs. The face of the queen was radiant with joy. The king seemed a little embarrassed, but very triumphant. The Duchess of Savoy betrayed alternately surprise, indignation, and despair. The eagle eye and painful experience of Mary taught her that the Princess Marguerite was struggling to retain her self-possession, and to maintain a cheerful spirit, while some terrible blow had fallen upon her.

The news from Spain was such that Mazarin, upon receiving it after midnight, hastened to the bedchamber of the queen with the announcement. As he entered, the queen rose upon her pillow, and the cardinal said:

"I have come to tell you, madame, a piece of news which your majesty never anticipated."

"Is peace proclaimed?" inquired the queen, earnestly.

"More than peace," the cardinal exultantly replied; "for the Infanta brings peace in her hand as but a portion of her dower."

This extraordinary scene took place on the night of the 29th of November, 1658. It was the task of the wily cardinal to break the humiliating intelligence to the Duchess of Savoy. He assured her that he felt bound to seek, above all things else, the interests of France; that an opportunity had unexpectedly occurred for an alliance with Spain; that this alliance was far more desirable than any other; but that, should any thing occur to interrupt these negotiations, he would do every thing in his power to promote the marriage of the king with the Princess Marguerite.

Notwithstanding the intense irritation which this communication excited, there was too much self-respect and too much good breeding in the court of Savoy to allow of a sudden rupture, which would provoke the sarcastic remarks of the world. Still the duchess, in a private interview with Mazarin, could not restrain her feelings, but broke out into passionate upbraidings. The thought that she had been lured to expose herself and her daughter to the derision of all Europe stung her to the quick. The Princess Marguerite, however, by her graceful composure, by her courtesy to all around her, and by the skill with which she concealed her wounded feelings, won the admiration of all in both courts.

For several days the two courts remained together, engaged in a round of festivities. This seemed necessary to avoid the appearance of an open rupture. The fickle king, in these assemblies, treated Marguerite with his customary courtesy; but he immediately turned to Mary Mancini with his marked attentions and devotion, dancing with her repeatedly on the same evening, and keeping her constantly by his side. Indeed, his attentions were so very marked as to lead the courtiers to think that the king rejoiced at his escape from his marriage with Marguerite from the hope that it might yet lead to his securing Mary for his bride. But it is more probable that the king, utterly selfish, reckless of the feelings of others, and devoted to his own enjoyment, sought the society of Mary because it so happened that she was the one, more than any other then within his reach, who, by her personal beauty and her mental attractions, could best beguile his weary hours. He was ready at any moment, without a pang, to lay her aside for another who could better minister to his pleasure or to the aspirings of his ambition.

The king, with his court, returned to Paris. The secret communicated by the mysterious visitor from Spain was still undivulged. The mystery was so great, and its apparent bearing upon the destiny of Mary so direct, that she resolved to interrogate one of the most influential ministers of the court upon the subject. He, thinking in some degree to evade the question, replied that the courier had come simply to inform Anne of Austria that the Queen of Spain had given birth to a son. This revealed the whole to Mary.

In the mean time, arrangements were made for Cardinal Mazarin to meet the Spanish minister on the frontiers of the two kingdoms to negotiate for the Spanish marriage. The cardinal, fully convinced that now it would be impossible to secure the hand of the king for his niece Mary, and anxious to convince the queen that he was heartily engaged in promoting the Spanish alliance, ordered Mary immediately to withdraw from the court, and retire to Brouage. This was a fortified town on the sea-coast many leagues from Paris. The king heard of the arrangement, and, forbidding the departure of Mary from the court, hastened to the cardinal demanding an explanation. Mazarin informed him that the Infanta of Spain would be very indignant should she learn that, while he was making application for her hand, he was retaining near him one whom he had long treated with the most devoted and affectionate attentions; that her father, Philip IV., would be disgusted; that there would be a probable rupture of the negotiations; and that the desolating war between France and Spain would continue.

Louis declared that he should not allow his pleasure to be disturbed by such considerations. Roused by opposition, he went so far as to say that he was quite ready to carry on the war with Spain if that power so wished; that the war would afford him an opportunity to acquire glory in the eyes of his countrymen, and in that case he would marry Mary Mancini.

But the cardinal was fully conscious that neither the queen nor France would now submit to such an arrangement. He had with great skill retained his attitude of command over the young monarch, holding his purse and governing the realm, while the boy-king amused himself as a ballet-dancer and a play-actor. The cardinal remained inexorable. It is said that the king wept in the excess of his chagrin as he felt compelled to yield to the representations of his domineering minister. As he unfolded to him the miseries which would be inflicted, not only upon the kingdom, but upon the court, should the desolating and expensive war be protracted, the king threw himself upon a sofa, and buried his face in his hands in silent despair. It was decided that Mary should be exiled from the court.

The king, thwarted, vexed, wretched, repaired to the cabinet of his mother. They conversed for an hour together. As they retired from the cabinet, Madame de Motteville says, "the eyes of both were red with weeping. The orders were immediately issued for Mary's departure. She was to go with an elder sister and her governess. The morrow came; the carriage was at the door. Mary, having taken leave of the queen, repaired to the apartment of Louis to bid him adieu. She found him deluged in tears. Summoning all her resolution to maintain self-control, she held out her trembling hand, and said to him reproachfully, 'Sire, you are a king; you weep; and yet I go.'"

The king uttered not a word, but, burying his face in his hands upon the table, sobbed aloud. Mary saw that it was all over with her; that there was no longer any hope. Without speaking a word, she descended the stairs to her carriage. The king silently followed her, and stood by the coach door. She took her seat with her companions, and, without the interchange of a word or a sign, the carriage drove away. Louis remained upon the spot until it disappeared from sight.

[Illustration: ISLE OF PHEASANTS.]

The Isle of Pheasants, a small Spanish island in the Bidassoa, a boundary river between France and Spain, was fixed upon as the rendezvous for the contracting parties for the royal marriage. Four days after the exile of Mary, the king and court, with a magnificent civil and ecclesiastical retinue, set out for the island. The king insisted, notwithstanding the vehement remonstrances of the queen, upon visiting Mary Mancini on the journey. As the splendid cortège passed through the streets of Paris, the whole population was on the pavement, shouting a thousand blessings on the head of their young king.

Mary Mancini had received orders from the queen to proceed with her sister to Saint Jean d'Angély, where, upon the passage of the court, she was to have an interview with the king. "Her interview," writes Miss Pardoe, "was, however, a bitter one. Divided between vanity and affection, Louis was at once less firm and less self-possessed than Mary. He wept bitterly, and bewailed the fetters by which he was shackled. But as he remarked the change which nights of watching and of tears had made in her appearance, he felt half consoled. The only result of this meeting was to harrow the heart of the poor victim of political expediency, and to prove to her upon how unstable a foundation she had built her superstructure of hope."[G]

[Footnote G: Louis XIV. and the Court of France, vol. ii., p. 23, 24.]

From Saint Jean d'Angély the court proceeded, by way of Bordeaux, to Toulouse. Here they awaited the conclusion of the treaty. The negotiation was tedious, as each party was anxious to gain all that was possible from the other. Many questions of national moment and pride were involved. At length the conference was amicably concluded. The king agreed to pardon the Prince of Condé, and restore to him all his honors; and the Infanta Maria Theresa renounced for herself and her descendants all claim to the inheritance of her parents. She was to receive as a dowry five hundred thousand golden crowns. There were several other articles included in the treaty which have now ceased to be of any interest.

Much surprise was soon excited in the court of Louis XIV. by the intimation that the marriage ceremony must be postponed until the spring. Philip IV. stated that his infirm health would not allow him to take so long a journey in the inclement weather of winter. Louis XIV. had never yet seen his affianced bride. We do not learn that he was at all annoyed by the delay. The intervening weeks were passed in journeyings and a round of amusements. Early in May, 1660, the king returned to the vicinity of the Isle of Pheasants, where he was to meet the King of Spain and Maria Theresa.

The most magnificent preparations had been made at the Isle of Pheasants for the interview between the two courts and the royal nuptials. Bridges were constructed to the island from both the French and Spanish sides of the river. These bridges were covered, and so decorated as to present the aspect of beautiful galleries. Upon the island a palace was erected, consisting of one immense and gorgeous apartment, with lateral chambers and dressing-rooms. This apartment was carpeted, and furnished with all the splendor which the combined monarchies of France and Spain could command.

Two doors, directly opposite each other, enabled the two courts to enter simultaneously. A straight line across the centre of the room divided it into two portions, one half of which was regarded as French, and the other as Spanish territory. The Spanish court took up its residence at Fontarabia, on the eastern or Spanish bank of the river. Louis and his court occupied Saint Jean de Luz, on the French or western side of the stream.

There are many exactions of court etiquette which to republican eyes seem extremely irrational and foolish. Louis could not cross the river to take his Spanish bride, neither could Maria Theresa cross the stream to be married on French soil; therefore Don Luis de Haro, as the proxy of Louis XIV., having the French Bishop of Frejus as his witness, was married to Maria Theresa in the church at Fontarabia. The ceremony was conducted with the most punctilious observance of the stately forms of Spanish etiquette.

Madame de Motteville gives the following account of the appearance of the bride:

"The Infanta is short, but well made. We admired the extreme fairness of her complexion. The blue eyes appeared to us to be fine, and charmed us by their softness and brilliancy. We celebrated the beauty of her mouth, and of her somewhat full and roseate lips. The outline of her face is long, but, being rounded at the chin, pleased us. Her cheeks, rather large, but handsome, had their share of our praise. Her hair, of a very light auburn, accorded admirably with her fine complexion."

The Infanta was dressed in white satin, ornamented with small bows of silver serge. She wore a large number of brilliant gems, and her head was decorated with a mass of false hair. The first lady of her household bore her train.

During the ceremony Philip IV. stood between his daughter and the proxy of Louis. The princess did not present her hand to Don Luis, nor did he present to her the nuptial ring. At the close of the ceremony the father embraced his child, and silently the gorgeous train swept from the church.

The next day Anne of Austria, accompanied by her second son, then Duke of Orleans, repaired to the Isle of Pheasants to meet her brother, Philip IV., and the royal bride. Court etiquette did not yet allow Louis XIV. to have an interview with the lady to whom he was already married by proxy. He, however, sent to his young queen, by one of his nobles, a present of some very fine jewels.

Though Philip IV. was the brother of Anne of Austria, and though they had not met for many years, Spanish etiquette would not allow any demonstrations of tenderness. The interview was chillingly stately and dignified. Anne, for a moment forgetting the icy restraints of the court, in sisterly love endeavored to salute her brother on the cheek. The Spanish king held back his head, rejecting the proffered fondness. The young bride threw herself upon her knees, requesting permission to kiss the hand of Anne of Austria. The queen-mother lifted her from the floor, and tenderly embraced her.

After some time had elapsed, Cardinal Mazarin entered, of course from the French side, and, advancing to their majesties, informed them that there was a distinguished stranger at the door who begged permission to enter. Anne and Philip affected to hold a brief conference upon the subject, when they gave their consent for his admission.

Louis XIV. entered in regal attire to see for the first time, and to be seen for the first time by, his bride. As he approached, Maria Theresa fixed her eyes upon him, and blushed deeply. Philip IV. smiled graciously, and said audibly to

Anne of Austria, "I have a very handsome son-in-law."

As we have mentioned, there was a line separating the Spanish half of the room from the French half. Louis advanced to the centre of the apartment, and kneeled upon a cushion which had been provided for him there. The King of Spain kneeled also upon a similar cushion. Cardinal Mazarin then brought in a Bible, with a cross upon the volume. One of the high Spanish church officials did the same on his side. The treaty of peace was then read simultaneously to Philip IV. in Spanish, to Louis XIV. in French. At its conclusion, they each placed their hands upon the Bible, and took a solemn oath to observe its stipulations. During this scene one sovereign was ceremonially in France, and the other in Spain. Having taken the oath, they rose, and in stately strides advanced to the frontier line. Here they cordially embraced each other.

At the conclusion of sundry other ceremonies, some tedious, some imposing, the two courts returned each to its own side of the river. Maria Theresa accompanied her father. The next morning the queen-mother, with a suitable retinue, returned to the island palace, where she met again the bride of her son, and conducted her to her own apartments at Saint Jean de Luz. Two days elapsed, while preparations were made again to solemnize the marriage beneath the skies of France.

A platform was constructed, richly carpeted, from the residence of Anne of Austria to the church. The young maiden-queen was robed in French attire for this repetition of the nuptial ceremony. She wore a royal mantle of violet-colored velvet, sprinkled with fleur de lis, over a white dress. A queenly crown was upon her brow. Her gorgeous train was borne by three of the most distinguished ladies of France. At the conclusion of this ceremony Louis XIV. received his bride. The king was then in the twenty-second year of his age.

Until within a week of the royal marriage, the king wrote frequently to Mary Mancini. Then the correspondence was suddenly dropped. The king never after seemed to manifest any interest in her fate.

After a few days of festivity, the court commenced, on the 15th of June, its leisurely return toward Paris. Having reached Vincennes, the illustrious cortège tarried for several days in the royal chateau there, until preparations could be completed for a magnificent entrance into the capital. The gorgeous spectacle took place on the 26th of August, 1660. For many weeks the saloons of the Louvre and the Tuileries resounded with unintermitted revelry.

KARTINDO PUBLISHING HOUSE (Kartindo.Com)

[Illustration: THE LOUVRE AND THE TUILERIES.]

Very cruelly the queen-mother sent a message to Mary Mancini, expressing her regret that she could not be present at the royal nuptials, and requiring her to come immediately to be present at the entrée of the king and queen into the metropolis, and to share in the festivities of the palace. The order came to the crushed and bleeding heart of Mary like a death-summons. Accompanied by her two sisters, and with suitable attendants, she set forth on her sad journey. All France was rejoicing over the royal marriage, and as her carriage rapidly approached Paris, every hour pierced her heart with a new pang. With all the fortitude she could summon, she could not retain the roseate glow of health and happiness. Her cheeks were pale and emaciate, and her forced smile only proclaimed more loudly the grief which was consuming her heart. She alighted at the new palace of her uncle, Cardinal Mazarin, and hastily retired to her apartment.

She had scarcely entered her room ere a letter from the cardinal was presented to her, soliciting her hand for Prince Colonna, one of the most illustrious nobles in wealth and rank in Europe. This marriage would give her position scarcely second to that of any lady not seated on a throne. The ambitious cardinal, not fully understanding the delicate mechanism of a young lady's heart, had negotiated this matter, hoping thus to rescue his niece from the humiliating sympathy of the courtiers. But the noble nature of Mary recoiled from such a rescue. She had instinctively resolved that in her own person, and by her own individual force of character, however great might be her sufferings, she would maintain her womanly dignity. Consequently, to the surprise of the cardinal, she returned a cold and positive refusal to the proposition.

Soon after this she received a communication to repair to the palace of Fontainebleau, there to be presented to the young queen, with her two sisters, and many others of the notabilities of the realm. The presentation was to take place on the ensuing Sunday, immediately after high mass. Her elder sister, the Countess de Soissons, assisted by the Princess de Conti, was to preside at the ceremony.

Mary had just entered the audience-hall, and was approaching the queen to be presented, when Louis XIV. entered the apartment to invite Maria Theresa to accompany him in a walk in the park. Just at that moment Madame de Soissons was presenting Mademoiselle *Mancini*. The king heard the name which had once been apparently so dear to him. Without the slightest emotion or the least sign of recognition, he bowed, as if in the presence of a perfect stranger, and inquired of Mary respecting her uncle the cardinal. He then exchanged a few courteous words with the other ladies in the room with the same assumed or real indifference, and invited all the ladies of the circle to attend the queen in a hunt in which she was about to engage.

It seemed as if the fates had combined to expose poor Mary to every species of mental torture. Her brain reeled, and, scarcely able to retain her footing, she withdrew a little apart to rally her disordered senses. Unable any longer to endure these sufferings, she begged to be excused from attending the hunt, alleging that the feeble health of her uncle the cardinal rendered it necessary for her to return to Paris. Her carriage was ordered for her departure, but, at a short distance from the chateau, she encountered the whole hunting-party, filling the road with its splendor. Her carriage was compelled to stop, that the king and queen and royal train might pass.

"And thus again she saw Louis, who preceded the cavalcade on horseback, surrounded by the nobles of his court. The heart of Mary throbbed almost to bursting. It was impossible that the king should not recognize the livery of her uncle--the carriage in which he had so often been seated by her side; he would not, he *could* not pass her by without one word. She deceived herself. His majesty was laughing at some merry tale, by which he was so much engrossed that he rode on without even bestowing a look upon the gilded coach and its heart-broken occupant."[H]

[Footnote H: Louis XIV. and the Court of France, vol. ii., p. 48.]

Mary returned to Paris pondering deeply her awful destiny. She saw that she was fated to meet continually the king and queen in their festivities; that with a broken heart she must feign gayety and smiles; that by lingering torture she must sink into the grave. There was no refuge for her but to escape from Paris and from the court. Apparently the only way to accomplish this was to accept the proffered hand of the Prince Colonna, who would remove her from Paris to Rome.

[Illustration: PALACE OF FONTAINEBLEAU.]

The next morning, pale and tearless, Mary drove to Vincennes, where Cardinal Mazarin then was, and informed him that she was ready to marry Prince Colonna, provided the marriage could take place immediately, and that the cardinal would, without an hour's delay, write to the king to obtain his consent.

The cardinal was rejoiced, and proceeded with energy. The king, without one kind word, gave his cold and indifferent consent. In accordance with the claims of etiquette, he sent her some valuable gifts, which she did not dare to decline.

"Mary walked to the altar," says Miss Pardoe, to whom we are indebted for many of these details, "as she would have walked to the scaffold, carrying with her an annual dower of one hundred thousand livres, and perjuring herself by vows which she could not fulfill. Her after career we dare not trace. Suffice it that the ardent and enthusiastic spirit which would, had she been fated to happiness, have made her memory a triumph for her sex, embittered by falsehood, wrong, and treachery, involved her in errors over which both charity and propriety oblige us to draw a veil; and if all Europe rang with the enormity of her excesses, much of their origin may safely be traced to those who, after wringing her heart, trampled it in the dust beneath their feet."

A few days after the scenes of presentation at Fontainebleau, the royal pair made their triumphal entry into Paris. In those days of feudal oppression and ignorance, the masses looked up to kings and queens with a degree of superstitious reverence which, in our enlightened land, seems almost inconceivable. Louis XIV. was a heartless, selfish, pleasure-loving young man of twenty-one, who had never in his life done any thing to merit the especial esteem of any one. Maria Theresa was an amiable and pretty girl, who never dreamed that she had any other function than to indulge in luxuries at the expense of others. Millions were to be impoverished that she and her husband might pass through life reveling in luxury and charioted in splendor. One can not contemplate such a state of things without being agitated by the conflicting emotions of pity for such folly and indignation for such outrages. Louis and Maria Theresa were received by the populace of Paris with as much reverence and enthusiasm as if they had been angels descending from heaven, fraught with every blessing.

Scarcely had the morning dawned ere the whole city was in commotion. The streets were thronged with countless thousands in the most brilliant gala dresses. Triumphal arches spanned the thoroughfares through which the royal procession was to pass. Garlands of flowers and hangings of brilliantly colored tapestry concealed the fronts of the houses from view. The pavements were strewn with flowers and sweet-scented herbs, over which the wheels of the carriages and the hoofs of the horses would pass without noise. At the barrier a gorgeous throne was erected. Here the young queen was seated in royal state, to receive the homage of the several distinguished officers of the city and of the realm. At the close of these ceremonies, which were rendered as imposing as

KARTINDO PUBLISHING HOUSE (Kartindo.Com)

civil and ecclesiastical pomp could create, the apparently interminable procession of carriages, and horsemen, and footmen, with the most dazzling adornments of caparisons, and uniforms, and banners, with resounding music, and shouts of acclaim which seemed to rend the skies, commenced its entrance into the city.

An antique car had been constructed, of massive and picturesque proportions, emblazoned with gold. Upon this car the young queen was seated. She was, in reality, very beautiful, but in this hour of triumph, with flushed cheek and sparkling eye, robed in the richest attire, brilliant with gems, and so conspicuously enthroned as to be visible to every eye, she presented an aspect of almost celestial loveliness.

The young king rode by her side, magnificently mounted. His garments of velvet, richly embroidered with gold and jewels, had been prepared for the occasion at an expense of considerably more than a million of dollars. The splendors of this gala-day were never forgotten by those who witnessed them.

For succeeding weeks and months the court luxuriated in one continued round of gayety and extravagance. Night after night the magnificent saloons of the Louvre and the Tuileries resounded with music, while proud lords and high-born dames trod the floors in the mazy dance, and inflamed their passions with the most costly wines. It can not be denied that a man who is trained from infancy amidst such scenes could acquire elegance of manner which those engrossed in the useful and ennobling employments of life rarely attain. Neither can it be denied that this is as poor a school as can possibly be imagined to prepare one wisely to administer the affairs of a nation of twenty millions of people. In fact, Louis XIV. never dreamed of consulting the interests of the people. It was his sole object to aggrandize himself by promoting the splendor, the power, and the glory of the monarchy.

One does well to be angry when he reflects that, to maintain this reckless and utterly useless extravagance of the king and the court, the millions of the peasantry of France were compelled to live in mud hovels, to wear the coarsest garb, to eat the plainest food, while their wives and their daughters toiled barefooted in the fields. One would think that guilty consciences would often be appalled by the announcement, "Know thou that for all these things God will bring thee into judgment?"

Though this revolting state of society was the slow growth of time, and though no one there could have regarded this aristocratic oppression as it is now estimated in the clearer light of the present day, still these outrages, inflicted by the strong upon the weak, by the rich upon the poor, merit the unmitigated condemnation of men, as they have ever incurred the denunciations of God.

Cardinal Mazarin, more than any other man in France, was accountable for the enormous luxury of the court, and the squalid misery of the people. He knew better. He was professedly a disciple of Jesus Christ, and yet a more thorough worldling could hardly have been in Christian or in pagan lands. He was one of the most gigantic robbers of the poor of which history gives any mention.

In the midst of these festivities, Mazarin decided to invite the court to a grand ballet, which should transcend in splendor every thing which Paris had witnessed before. To decorate the saloons, a large amount of costly draperies were manufactured at Milan. In arranging these tapestries, by some accident they took fire. The flames spread rapidly, utterly destroying the room, with its paintings and its magnificently frescoed roof. The fire was eventually extinguished, but the shock was a death-blow to the cardinal. He was then in feeble health. His attendants conveyed him from the blazing room to the Chateau Mazarin.

The terror of the scene so aggravated the maladies from which the cardinal had for a long time suffered, that he was prostrated upon his bed, and it soon became evident that his dying hour was near at hand. There are many indications that the haughty cardinal was tortured by the pangs of remorse. He was generally silent, though extremely dejected. His body was subjected to the most extraordinary convulsions, while inaudible murmurs escaped his lips.

Count de Brienne, in his memoirs, states that, on one occasion, he entered the chamber of the cardinal on tiptoe, his valet informing him that his eminence was asleep. He found Mazarin bolstered in an arm-chair before the fire, apparently in a profound slumber, "and yet," writes the count, "his body rocked to and fro with the greatest rapidity, from the back of his chair to his knees, now swinging to the right, and again to the left. These movements of the sufferer were as regular and rapid as the vibrations of the pendulum of a clock. At the same time inarticulate murmurs escaped his lips."

The count, much moved by the wretched spectacle, summoned the attendant, and awoke the cardinal. Mazarin, in awaking, betrayed that troubled state of soul which had thus agitated his body. In most melancholy tones, he said,

"My physician, M. Guénaud, has informed me that I can live but a few days."

Count de Brienne, wishing to console him, said, "But M. Guénaud is not omniscient. He may be deceived."

The cardinal, uttering a heavy sigh, exclaimed, "Ah! M. Guénaud well understands his trade."

Mazarin, as we have mentioned, had acquired enormous wealth. The resources of the kingdom had been in his hands. The poor had been oppressed by as terrible a system of taxation as human nature could endure and live. With the sums thus extorted, he had not only maintained the army, and supported the voluptuousness of the court, but he had also appropriated vast sums, without the slightest right to do so, to his own private enrichment. He was now dying. The thought of going to the bar of God with his hands full of this stolen gold tortured him. Constrained by the anguish of a death-bed, he sent for a Theatine monk to act as his confessor, and to administer, in his last hours, the services of the Church.

The virtuous monk was quite startled when the cardinal, with pale and trembling lips, informed him that he had accumulated a fortune of over forty millions of francs--$8,000,000. Mazarin allowed that he considered it a sin that he had by such means accumulated such vast wealth. His pious confessor boldly declared that the cardinal would peril his eternal salvation if he did not, before his death, make restitution of all his ill-gotten gains, reserving only that for which he was indebted to the bounty of the king.

The dying sinner, trembling in view of the judgment, replied in faltering accents, "In that case I must relinquish all. I have received nothing from the king. My family must be left in utter beggary."

The confessor was deeply moved by the aspect of despair presented by the cardinal. Embarrassed by the difficulties of the position, he sent for a distinguished member of the court, M. Colbert, to confer with upon the situation.

The shrewd courtier, after a little deliberation, suggested that, as it would be manifestly impossible to restore the money to the different individuals, scattered all over the realm, from whom it had been gathered in the ordinary collection of the taxes, the cardinal should make a transfer of it, as a donation, to the sovereign. "The king," added M. Colbert, "will, without any question, annul so generous an act, and restore the property to you. It will then be yours by royal grant."

The cardinal, who had lived, and moved, and had his being in the midst of trickery and intrigue, highly approved of the suggestion. The papers were immediately made out, transferring the property to the king. It was the 3d of March, 1661. Three days passed, and there was no response of rejection--no recognition of the gift. The cardinal was terror-stricken. As he sat bolstered in his chair, he wrung his hands in agony, often exclaiming, "My poor family! my poor family! they will be left without bread."

At the close of the third day M. Colbert entered the dying chamber with a document in his hand, announcing that the king had restored to the cardinal all his property, authorizing him to dispose of it as he judged to be best.

It is scarcely possible that this trickery could have satisfied the conscience of the cardinal. His confessor professed to be satisfied, and granted the dying man that absolution which he had previously withheld. Still Mazarin was extremely reluctant to die. He dressed with the utmost care; painted his wrinkled brow and emaciate cheeks, and resorted to all the appliances of art to maintain the aspect of youth and vigor. But death could not thus be deceived. The destroying angel on the 9th of March bore his spirit away to the judgment seat of Christ. He died in the Chateau Mazarin, at the age of fifty-two, having been virtually monarch of France for eighteen years.

[Illustration: CHATEAU MAZARIN.]

It appeared by the will of Mazarin that his property was vastly greater even than the enormous sum which he had reluctantly admitted. That portion of it which might be included under the term real estate, consisting of houses, lands, etc., amounted to over fifty millions of francs, while his personal effects, embracing the most costly furniture, diamonds, and other jewels, of which he strictly forbade any inventory to be taken, amounted to many millions more. The legacies to his nieces and to other aristocratic friends were truly princely. To the *poor* he left a miserable pittance amounting to about twelve hundred dollars.

The cardinal was a heartless, avaricious man, of but little ability, and yet endowed with a very considerable degree of that cunning which sometimes proves to be temporarily so successful in diplomatic intrigues. The king was probably glad to be rid of him, for he could not easily throw off a yoke to which he had been habituated from childhood. During most of the cardinal's illness Louis continued his usual round of feasting and dancing. Upon his death he manifested no grief. It seems that he had previously made up his mind no longer to be troubled by a prime minister, but to rule absolutely by his own will.

Two days before the death of Mazarin, when he was no longer capable of transacting any business, the president of the ecclesiastical assembly inquired of the king "to whom he must hereafter address himself on questions of public business." The emphatic and laconic response was, "*To myself.*"

CHAPTER V

FESTIVITIES OF THE COURT

1661-1664

Influence and reputation of Mazarin.--Character of M. Fouquet.--Information given by M. Colbert.--Appearance of Louis XIV.--Charles II., King of England, and family.--The Princess Henrietta.--Marriage of Philip.--Fascinations of Henrietta.--Grief of Maria Theresa.--The queen-mother appealed to.--Mademoiselle de la Vallière.--Visit to the palace of Blois.--Fascination of Louis.--Louise captivated.--Festivities at Fontainebleau.--Discussion of the court ladies.--Vexation of Louise.--Discovery by Louis.--Louis and Mademoiselle de Vallière.--Sudden interruption of festivities.--Attentions of Louis.--Anecdote.--The lottery and the bracelets.--The palace of Vaux.--Splendor of the palace.--Rebuke of Louis.--Magnificent scenes.--Continued festivities.--Significant motto.--Fouquet in danger.--Intervention of Louise.--M. Fouquet imprisoned.--Continued gayety at court.--Important dispatches.--The king's orders.--Relationship of the French and Spanish courts.--The apology of Philip IV.--Conduct of M. Créqui.--The Pope humbled.--Remorse of de la Vallière.--Illness of Anne of Austria.--Trials of Mademoiselle de la Vallière.--Disappointment.--Flight of Mademoiselle de la Vallière.--Seeks admission to the convent, and is denied.--Reproaches of the queen-mother.--Fury of Louis.--Power of Louis over Mademoiselle de la Vallière.--Return of Mademoiselle de la Vallière to the court.--Reinstated.--Resolve of Louis.--Versailles.--Extravagance of the king.--Magnificent fêtes.

Cardinal Mazarin was exceedingly unpopular both with the court and the masses of the people. Haughty, domineering, avaricious, there was nothing in his character to win the kindly regards of any one. His death gave occasion to almost universal rejoicing. Indeed, it was with some difficulty that the king repressed the unseemly exhibition of this joy on the part of the court. The cardinal, as we have mentioned, had been for many years virtually monarch of France. He, in the name of the king, imposed the taxes, appointed the ministry, issued all orders, and received all reports. The accountability was so entire to him that the monarch, immersed in pleasure, had but little to do with reference to the affairs of the realm.

KARTINDO PUBLISHING HOUSE (Kartindo.Com)

Immediately upon the death of Mazarin, the king summoned to his presence Tellier, minister of War, Lionne, minister of State, and Fouquet, minister of the Treasury. He informed them that he should continue them in office, but that henceforth he should dispense with the services of a prime minister, and that they would be responsible to him alone. The young king was then twenty-two years of age. He was very poorly educated, had hitherto developed no force of character, and appeared to all to be simply a frivolous, pompous, self-conceited young man of pleasure.

Fouquet had held the keys of the treasury. When the king needed money he applied to him for a supply. The almost invariable reply he received was,

"Sire, the treasury is empty, but his eminence will undoubtedly advance to your majesty a loan."

The money came, the king little cared where from while reveling in luxury, and dancing and flirting with the beauties who crowded his court.

Fouquet was an able but thoroughly unprincipled man. He had grown enormously rich by robbing the treasury. The king disliked him. But Fouquet knew that the king could not dispense with his services. He was a marvelously efficient financier, and well knew how to wrench gold from the hands of the starving millions. The property he had acquired by fraud was so great that he often outvied the king in the splendor of his establishments. Conscious of his power, he doubted not that he should still be able to hold the king, in a measure, subject to his control.

Scarcely had Louis returned from his brief conference with his ministers to his cabinet at the Louvre, ere the secretary of the deceased cardinal, M. Colbert, entered, and requested a private audience. He informed the king, to his astonishment and inexpressible delight, that the cardinal had concealed fifteen millions of money (three millions of dollars) in addition to the sums mentioned in his will; that it was doubtless his intention that this money should immediately replenish the utterly exhausted treasury of his majesty.

The king was overjoyed. He could scarcely believe the intelligence. Concealing the tidings from Fouquet, he speedily and secretly recovered the money from the several places in which it had been deposited. Fifteen millions of francs would be a large sum at any time, but two hundred years ago it was worth three or four times as much as now. Fouquet was utterly bewildered in attempting to imagine where the king had obtained the sums he was so lavishly expending.

Louis XIV. by nature and by education was excessively fond of the pomp and the punctilios of court etiquette. As this new era of independence dawned upon him, it was his first and most anxious object to regulate even to the minutest details the ceremonies of the court. He was of middling stature. High-heeled shoes added between two and three inches to his height. His hair was very fine and abundant, and he wore it long, in masses of ringlets upon his shoulders. Deep blue eyes, a fair complexion, and well moulded features formed an unusually handsome countenance. He was stately in his movements, pompous in his utterance, and every word of every sentence was pronounced slowly and with distinct enunciation, as if an oracle were giving out its responses.

There was no resemblance morally, intellectually, or physically between the king and his only brother Philip. They did not love each other. During their whole lives there had been one perpetual struggle on the part of the king to domineer over his brother, and on the part of Philip to resist that domination. Philip was gentle in disposition, effeminate in manners, and, though a voluptuary in his tastes, a man of chivalric courage. As Duke of Orleans he had large wealth, many retainers, and feudal privileges, which invested him with power which even the king was compelled to respect.

Charles II. was now King of England. The whole nation had apparently received him with exultation. Suddenly, from being a penniless and crownless wanderer, he had become a sovereign, second in rank and power to no other sovereign in Europe. His mother Henrietta, his widowed sister the Princess of Orange, and his younger sister Henrietta, of course, shared in the prosperity and elevation of Charles. They were no longer pensioners upon the charity of their French relatives, but composed the royal family of the British court.

It will be remembered how cruelly Louis treated his young cousin in the ball-room in the days of her adversity. Charles in those days had solicited of Mazarin the hand of his niece, Mary Mancini. But the proud cardinal promptly rejected the offer of a wandering prince, without purse or crown. Very soon after Charles II. ascended the throne of England, Mazarin hastened to inform him that he was ready to confer upon him his niece. Charles, a profligate fellow, declined the proffered alliance, to the great chagrin of the haughty cardinal.

Prosperity is sometimes a great beautifier. The young Princess Henrietta, upon

KARTINDO PUBLISHING HOUSE (Kartindo.Com)

whom the sun of prosperity was now shining in all its effulgence, seemed like a new being, radiantly lovely and self reliant. Philip fell desperately in love with her. With a form of exquisite symmetry, with the fairest complexion and lovely features, she suddenly found herself the sister of a monarch, transformed into the principal ornament, almost the central attraction, of the court. She went to England to attend the coronation of her brother. She then returned to Paris. On the 31st of March, 1661, she was married to Philip in the Palais Royal, in the presence of the royal family and the prominent members of the court.

A few weeks after this the whole court removed to Fontainebleau. Here a month was spent in an incessant round of festivities. The fickle king, as soon as his brother had married Henrietta, saw in her new personal beauty and mental charms. It is not improbable that she almost unconsciously, in order to avenge the past neglect of the king, had studied all courtly graces, all endearments of manner, all conversational charms, that she might compel the king to do justice to the fascinations of person and character with which she was conscious of being richly endowed. Unhappily, she was triumphantly successful; perhaps far more so than she had intended. The changeful and susceptible king became completely entranced. He was continually by her side, exasperating Philip by his gallantry, and keenly wounding the feelings of his young queen.

The marriage of the king with Maria Theresa had been merely a matter of state policy. The connection had not been inspired by any ardent affection on either side. Though the king treated her with great politeness as the Queen of France, her enthusiastic nature claimed a warmer sentiment from her young husband. When she saw the attentions to which she was entitled lavished upon Henrietta, the wife of his brother, her affectionate heart was chilled. She became reserved, wept, sought retirement, withdrawing from all those gayeties in which her husband attracted the attention of the whole court by his undisguised admiration for Henrietta. At last her secret anguish so far overcame her that she threw herself, trembling and in tears, at the feet of Anne of Austria, and confided to her the grief of her heart.

The queen-mother could not have been surprised at this avowal. Her eyes were open to that which all the court beheld; and, besides, Philip had already complained to his mother that Louis was endeavoring to rob him of the love of his bride. The remonstrances of the queen-mother were of no avail. The selfish king, ever seeking only his own pleasure, cared little for the wreck of the happiness of others. He devoted himself with increasing assiduity to the society of Henrietta, frequently held his court in her apartments, and instituted a series of magnificent fêtes in her honor.

KARTINDO PUBLISHING HOUSE (Kartindo.Com)

Philip, then Duke of Orleans, and in the enjoyment of magnificent revenues and of much independent feudal power as brother of the king, was designated in the court as *Monsieur*. There was at that time in the court a young lady, one of Henrietta's maids of honor, Mademoiselle de la Vallière. Her romantic career, which subsequently rendered her famous throughout Europe, merits a brief digression.

Louise Françoise, daughter of the Marquis de la Vallière, was born at Tours in the year 1644. She was, consequently, seventeen years of age at the time of which we write. Her father died in her infancy. Her mother, left with an illustrious name and a small income, took for a second husband a member of the court, Gaston, duke of Orleans, to whom we have previously alluded, who was brother of Louis XIII. and uncle of the king. He resided at Blois.

As the king and court were on their way to the frontiers of Spain for the marriage of Louis with Maria Theresa, it will be remembered that he stopped for a short visit to his uncle at his magnificent palace of Blois. This grand castle, with its gorgeous architectural magnificence, its shaded parks and blooming gardens, was to Louise and her many companions an earthly paradise. Here, in an incessant round of pleasures, she had passed her girlhood.

The sight of the young monarch, so graceful in figure, so handsome in features, so marvelously courteous in bearing, aroused all the enthusiasm of the susceptible young maiden of sixteen. He was her sovereign, as well as to her eyes the most fascinating specimen of a man. She felt as though she were gazing upon a superior, almost a celestial being. She dreamed not of having fallen in love with him. The feeling of admiration, and almost of adoration, was altogether too elevated for earthly passion. In the presence of the king she was but an obscure child. In the crowded assemblage of wealth, and rank, and beauty which greeted the king at Blois, Louise was unnoticed. The king went on his way, leaving an impression on the heart of the young girl which could never be effaced. She thought it would be heaven to live in his presence, to watch his movements, to listen to his words, even though no word were addressed to her.

Soon after this the Duke of Orleans died. His court was broken up. Louise was appointed to a place as one of the maids of honor of the Princess Henrietta. She joined the court of *Madame* in Paris just before their departure for Fontainebleau, to which place, of course, she accompanied them.

KARTINDO PUBLISHING HOUSE (Kartindo.Com)

Here, in the midst of scenes of most brilliant festivities, Louise feasted her eyes with the sight of the king. Louis was exceedingly fond of exhibiting his grace as a dancer. Among these entertainments, the king took part in a ballet with Henrietta, he, in very picturesque dress, representing the goddess Ceres. At the close of the ballet, Louise, bewildered by the scene, and oppressed by inexplicable emotions, proposed to three of her lady companions that they should take a short walk into the dim recesses of the forest. It was a brilliant night, and the cool breeze fanned their fevered cheeks. As the four young ladies retired, one of the companions of the king laughingly suggested to him that they should follow them, and learn the secret of their hearts.

The ladies seated themselves at the foot of a large tree, where they began to discuss the scenes and actors of the evening. The king and his companion, concealed at a short distance, heard every word they uttered. Louise was for a time silent, but, being appealed to upon some subject, with very emphatic utterance remarked that she wondered that they could see any body, or think of any body but the king, when he was present. Upon her companions rallying her for being so much carried away by the splendors of royalty, she declared "that it was not the king, as a *king*, who excited her admiration, but it was Louis, as the most perfect of men; that his crown added nothing to his splendor of person or mind."

The king could not see the speaker; he could only hear her enthusiastic and impassioned voice. The parties returned to the chateau. Louise was very much chagrined that she should have allowed herself so imprudently to express her feelings. She knew that the conversation would be repeated, and feared that she should become a subject of ridicule for the whole court. In the interesting account which she gives of these events in her autobiography, she says that she retired to her room and wept bitterly.

The next morning Louise repaired to the apartments of Henrietta. She was surrounded by her suite of ladies. The king was already there. As, with his accustomed gallantry, he passed down the room addressing a few words to each, he approached Louise. Her heart throbbed violently. He had never spoken to her before.

In response to his question, "And what did you think of the ballet last night?" she, greatly agitated, attempted an answer. The king observed her confusion, and instantly recognized her voice. It was the same which he had heard the evening before in the forest expressing such enthusiastic admiration for his person. The king started, and fixed his eyes so intently upon her as to increase her embarrassment and attract the observation of all around. With a profound bow the king passed on, but again and again was seen to turn his eyes to the blushing girl. From that time Mademoiselle de la Vallière became the object of the marked and flattering attention of the king.

The unaffected timidity and modesty of her demeanor, her brilliant complexion, large and languishing blue eyes, and profusion of flaxen hair, were enough of themselves to excite the admiration of one so enamored of beauty as was Louis XIV. But, in addition to this, the self-love of Louis was gratified by the assurance that Louise admired him for his personal qualities, and not merely for his kingly crown. As the king was well aware of the gossip with which the court was filled in view of his devotion to Madame Henrietta, he perhaps deemed it expedient, by special attention to Louise, to divert the current of thought and conversation.

A few days after this a great hunt took place in the park. It was a hot summer's day. At the close of the hunt a table was spread loaded with delicacies. As the king and the courtiers, in the keenest enjoyment of the merry scene, were partaking of the sumptuous repast, almost unobserved a thunder-cloud arose, and there descended upon them a flood of rain so deluging that the company scattered in all directions for shelter. Louise running, she knew not where, soon found the king by her side. Politely taking her by the hand, he hurried her to a large tree, whose dense canopy of leaves promised some protection from the shower. There they stood, the young and handsome king, the beautiful maiden, the rain falling upon them in floods. It is interesting to record that the homage which rank paid to beauty was such that the king stood bareheaded, with his plumed hat in his hand, engaged during the hour the rain descended in animated conversation. After this it was observed that in the evening drives in the park he would ride on horseback for a short time by the carriage of the queen, or of the Princess Henrietta, and would then gallop to the coach of Louise.

He soon commenced a daily correspondence with her. Louis was by no means a well-educated man. In fact, he might be almost regarded as illiterate; but his letters were written with so much delicacy of sentiment and elegance of expression, that Louise was embarrassed in knowing how to return suitable replies. She was mortified at the thought of having her awkward letters compared with the elegant epistles which she received. In her embarrassment, she applied to the Marquis of Dangeau, a man of superior talents and culture, to write her responses for her.

Louise was a very noble girl, frank, sincere, confiding. On one occasion, when the king was complimenting her upon the rare beauty of her letters, the artless child confessed that she was not the author of them, but that they were written by the Marquis of Dangeau. The king smiled, and had the grace to admit that his letters to her were written by the same individual!

It had become a common entertainment of the court to put up in a lottery some beautiful article of jewelry. On one occasion the king drew a very costly pair of bracelets. All were looking with some curiosity to see to whom he would present them. Pausing for a moment, the king admiringly contemplated the sparkling gems, and then, threading his way through the throng of ladies, advanced to Mademoiselle de la Vallière, who stood a little apart, and placed them in her hands. Henrietta turned pale, and bit her lip with vexation. The queen, Maria Theresa, looked on with a marble smile, which revealed nothing of her feelings. Louise was embarrassed, but with admirable tact she assumed that the king had merely presented them to her for inspection. After carefully examining them, she handed them back to him, saying, with a courtesy, "They are indeed very beautiful." Louis, instead of receiving them, said, with a stately bow, "In that case, mademoiselle, they are in hands too fair to resign them," and returned to his seat.

As we have mentioned, the minister of the treasury was rolling in ill-gotten wealth. His palace of Vaux,[I] upon which he had expended fifteen millions of francs, eclipsed in splendor the royal palaces of Fontainebleau and Saint Germain. The king disliked him as a man. He knew very well that he was robbing the treasury, and it was annoying to have a subject live in state surpassing that of the sovereign. M. Fouquet very imprudently invited Louis and all his court to a magnificent fête at his chateau. All the notabilities of France were bidden to this princely festival, which the minister resolved should surpass, in splendor, any thing that France had hitherto witnessed.

[Footnote I: The chateau of Vaux was a spacious and magnificent palace in the small village of Maincy, about three miles from Melun. M. Fouquet purchased it, and expended enormous sums in enlarging the buildings, ornamenting the gardens, and decorating the walls with paintings. His expenditures were so lavish that the chateau exceeded in magnificence any of the royal palaces.]

The king, with an imposing escort, reached the gates of the chateau. Fouquet met him there, and conducted him and all the court, first, to the park. Here a spectacle of splendor presented itself which astonished the king. Notwithstanding all he had heard of the gorgeousness of his minister's palace, he was still not prepared for such a scene of luxury and enchantment. Instead of being gratified, he turned to Fouquet, and said to him bitterly,

"I shall never again, sir, venture to invite you to visit me. You would find yourself inconvenienced."

Fouquet felt the keen rebuke. For a moment he turned pale. He soon, however, rallied, and did all in his power to gratify his guests by the gorgeous spectacles and sumptuous entertainments of his more than regal home. The king, led by his host, passed through all the apartments of the chateau, and acknowledged that in its interior adornings there was not probably another edifice in Europe which could equal it in magnificence.

[Illustration: CHATEAU DE VAUX.]

In the evening there was a ball in the grand saloon of the castle. The king having danced several times with Louise, she became fatigued, and expressed the desire to leave, for a short time, the heated room. Louis drew her arm through his own, and, conducting her through the magnificent suite of apartments, which had already excited his displeasure, pointed out to her the armorial bearings of the proud minister, which were conspicuous in every room. The shield represented a squirrel ascending the topmost branches of a tree, with the motto "*quo non ascendam.*"

Neither the king nor his fair companion understood Latin. Just then the king's secretary, M. Colbert, entered. He hated Fouquet. He had already detected the minister in many falsifications of the treasury accounts, and had explained the robbery to the king. Louis had been for some time contemplating the arrest of Fouquet, but hardly dared, as yet, to strike one so powerful.

As M. Colbert entered, Louise inquired of him the significance of the motto.

"It signifies," he replied, "*to what height may I not attain*, and this significance is well understood by those who know the boldness of the squirrel or that of his master."

Just at that moment another courtier came up, who remarked, "Your majesty has probably not observed that in every instance the squirrel is pursued by a serpent."

KARTINDO PUBLISHING HOUSE (Kartindo.Com)

The king turned pale with anger, and ordered the captain of his musketeers to attend him. Louise understood full well what this meant. She threw herself at his feet, and entreated him not to sully his reputation by arresting a man whose guest he was, and who was entertaining him and his court with the highest honors. With the greatest difficulty, the king was dissuaded from immediate action. For a time he smothered his vengeance, and the court returned to Fontainebleau.

The king's displeasure not only remained unabated, but increased with added evidence of the pride, display, and fraudulent transactions of his minister. At length he ordered him to be secretly arrested, conveyed in close confinement to Angers, while a seal was placed on all his property. But for the interposition of the kind-hearted Louise, the degraded minister would have lost his life. It was easy for the king, immersed in pleasure, to forget the miserable. M. Fouquet was left in his imprisonment, almost as entirely lost to the world as if he had been consigned to the *oubliettes* of the Bastile.

Soon after this, the 1st of November, 1661, Maria Theresa gave birth to a dauphin. Louis was greatly elated. Still, the pride which he took in the child as the heir to the throne did not secure for his neglected wife any more tenderness of regard. He treated her with great courtesy, while his affections were vibrating between Henrietta and Louise. Every thing seemed to combine to magnify the power of the king. Still, the pleasure-loving monarch, while apparently wholly resigning himself to the career of a voluptuary, was with instinctive sagacity striving to undermine the resources of the haughty nobility, and to render his own court the most magnificent in Europe.

For several months the court continued immersed in gayety. Dancing, in all variety of costumes, was the great amusement of the king. There were balls every evening. Mademoiselle de la Vallière became more and more the object of the marked attentions of Louis. All his energies seemed absorbed in the small-talk of gallantry; still there were occasional indications that there were latent forces in the mind of the king which events might yet develop.

One evening the king was attending a brilliant ball in the apartments of Henrietta. As he was earnestly engaged in conversation with the beautiful Louise, some important dispatches were placed in his hands. He seated himself at a table to examine them. Many eyes watched his countenance as he silently perused the documents. It was observed at one moment that he turned deadly pale, and bit his lip with vexation. Having read the dispatches to the end, he angrily crushed them in his hand, and said to several of the officers of the court who were around him,

"Our embassador in London has been publicly insulted by the Spanish embassador." Then turning to M. Tellier, the Minister of War, he said, "Let my embassador at Madrid leave that city immediately. Order the Spanish envoy to quit Paris within twenty-four hours. The conferences at Flanders are at an end. Unless Spain publicly recognizes the superiority of our crown, she may prepare for a renewal of the war."

These orders of the king created general consternation. It was virtually inaugurating another war, with all its untold horrors. M. Tellier seemed thunderstruck. The king, perceiving his hesitation, said to him imperiously,

"Do you not understand my orders? I wish you immediately to assemble the council. I will meet them in an hour."

The king then returned to the ladies, and entered into trifling small-talk with them, as if nothing of moment had occurred.

It seems that a dispute had arisen in London between the French and Spanish embassadors upon the point of precedence. This had led to a bloody encounter in the streets between the retinues of the two ministers. The French were worsted. The Spaniards gained the contested point.

The King of Spain was the brother of Anne of Austria. His first wife, the mother of Maria Theresa, was sister of Louis XIII., and consequently aunt of Louis XIV. Thus there was a peculiar bond of relationship between the French and Spanish courts. Still Louis was unrelenting in the vigorous action upon which he had entered. In addition to the hostile measures already adopted, a special messenger was sent to Philip IV. to inform him that, unless he immediately recognized the supremacy of the French court, and made a formal apology for the insult offered the French minister, war would ensue. The Spanish king, unwilling, for so trivial a cause, to involve the two nations in a bloody conflict, very magnanimously yielded to the requirements demanded by the hot blood and wounded pride of his son-in-law. In the presence of all the foreign ministers and the assembled court at Fontainebleau, the Spanish embassador made a humble apology, and declared that never again should the precedence of the embassador of France be denied.

A very similar difficulty occurred a short time after at Rome. The French embassador there, the Duke of Créqui, an old feudal noble, accompanied by troops of retainers armed to the teeth, had, by his haughty bearing, become extremely unpopular both with the court and the people of Rome. The myrmidons of the duke were continually engaged in night-brawls with the police. On one occasion they even attacked, sword in hand, the Pope's guard, and put them to flight. The brother of Pope Alexander VII., who hated Créqui, instigated the guard to take revenge. In an infuriated mob, they surrounded the palace of the embassador, and fired upon his carriage as it entered his court-yard. A page was killed, and several other attendants wounded. Créqui immediately left the city, accusing the Pope of instigating the outrage.

Louis XIV. demanded reparation, and the most humble apology. The proud Pope was not disposed to yield to his insolent demands. Affairs assumed so threatening an aspect, that the Pope ordered two of the guard, one an officer, to be hung, and the Mayor of Rome, who was accused of having instigated the outrage, to be banished. This concession, however, by no means satisfied the irascible Louis. He commenced landing troops in Italy, threatening to besiege Rome. The Pope appealed to the Roman Catholic princes of Germany for aid. They could not come to his rescue, for they were threatened with war by the Turks. The unhappy Pope was thus brought upon his knees. He was compelled to banish from Rome his own brother, Don Mario Chigi, and to send an embassador to Paris with the most humble apology.

These events were but slight episodes in the gay life of the pleasure-loving king. He was still reveling in an incessant round of feasting and dancing, flitting with his gay court from one to another of his metropolitan and rural palaces.

There are few so stern as not to feel emotions of sympathy rather than of condemnation for Louise de la Vallière. She was a child of seventeen, exposed to all the fascinations and temptations of the most luxurious court then upon the globe. But God has implanted in every bosom a sense of right and wrong. She wept bitterly over her fall. Her remorse was so great that she withdrew as far as possible from society, and the anguish of her repentance greatly embarrassed her royal lover.

Henrietta was greatly annoyed at the preference which the king had shown for Louise over herself. She determined to drive the unfortunate favorite from the court. Anne of Austria, with increasing years, was growing oblivious of her own youthful indiscretions, and was daily becoming more stern in her judgments. A cancer had commenced its secret ravages upon her person. Its progress no medical skill could arrest. She tried to conceal the terrible secret which was threatening her with the most loathsome and distressing of deaths. In this mood of mind the haughty queen sent for the weeping Louise to her room. Trembling in every nerve, the affrighted child attended the summons. She found Anne of Austria with Henrietta by her side. The queen, without assigning any cause, sternly informed her that she was banished from the court of France, and that suitable attendants would immediately convey her to a distant castle. Upon Louise attempting to make some inquiry why she was thus punished, the haughty queen sternly interrupted her with the reply "that France could not have two queens."

Louise staggered back to her room overwhelmed with despair. Both God and man will declare that, whatever fault there might have been in the relations then existing between the king and this unprotected girl, the censure should have rested a thousand fold more heavily upon the king than upon his victim. And yet Louise was to be driven in ignominy from the court, to enter into a desolated world utterly ruined. Through the remainder of the day no one entered her apartment. She spent the hours in tears and in the fever of despair. In the evening Louis himself came to her room and found her exhausted with weeping. He endeavored to ascertain the cause of her overwhelming distress. She, unwilling to be the occasion of an irreconcilable feud between the mother and the son, evaded all his inquiries. He resorted to entreaties, reproaches, threats, but in vain. Irritated by her pertinacious refusal, he suddenly left her without speaking a word of adieu.

Louise seemed now truly to be alone in the world, without a single friend left her. But she then recalled to mind that she had formerly entered into an agreement with the king that, in case of any misunderstanding arising between them, a night should not pass without an attempt at reconciliation. A new hope arose in her mind that the king would either return, or send her a note to inform her that his anger no longer continued.

"And so she waited and watched, and counted every hour as it was proclaimed from the belfry of the palace. But she waited and watched in vain. When at length, after this long and weary night, the daylight streamed through the silken curtains of her chamber, she threw herself upon her knees, and praying that God would not cast away the victim who was thus rejected by the world, she hastened, with a burning cheek and a tearless eye, to collect a few necessary articles of clothing, and throwing on her veil and mantle, rushed down a private staircase and escaped into the street. In this distracted state of mind she pursued her way to Chaillot,[J] and reached the convent of the Sisters of St. Mary, where she was detained some time in the parlor. At length the grating was opened and a portress appeared. On her request to be admitted to the abbess, she informed her that the community were all at their devotions, and could not see any one.

[Footnote J: Chaillot was a village on the banks of the Seine, about a mile and a half from the Tuileries, near the present bridge of Jena. The nuns of the order of St. Mary had a celebrated convent here, where persecuted grandeur often sought an asylum. Within the walls of this convent the widowed queen of Charles I. and daughter of Henry IV. died in the year 1669.]

"It was in vain that the poor fugitive entreated and asserted her intention of taking the vows. She could extort no other answer, and the portress withdrew, leaving her sitting on a wooden bench desolate, heart-sick. For two hours she remained motionless, with her eyes fixed upon the grating, but it continued closed. Even the dreary refuge of this poor and obscure convent was denied her. Even the house of religion had barred its doors against her. She could bear up no longer. From the previous evening she had not tasted food, and the fatigue of body and anguish of mind which she had undergone, combined with this unaccustomed fast, had exhausted her slight remains of strength. A sullen torpor gradually overcame her faculties, and eventually she fell upon the paved floor cold and insensible."[K]

[Footnote K: Louis XIV. and the Court of France, vol. ii., p. 125.]

The king had probably passed a very uncomfortable night. Early in the morning he learned that Louise had disappeared. Much alarmed, he hastened to the apartments of Madame Henrietta in the Tuileries. She unfeelingly expressed entire ignorance of the movements of Mademoiselle de la Vallière. He immediately repaired to the rooms of his mother. She was unable to give him any information respecting the lost favorite. Bitterly, however, she reproached her son with his want of self-control in allowing himself to cherish so strong an attachment to Mademoiselle de la Vallière. She accused him of having no mastery over himself.

The king's eyes flashed with indignation. He was fully convinced that his mother was in some way the cause of the departure of Louise. Angrily he replied,

"It may be so that I do not know how to control myself, but I will at least prove that I know how to control those who offend me."

Turning upon his heel, he left the apartment. By some means he obtained a clew to the retreat of Louise. Mounting his horse, accompanied by a single page, he galloped to the convent of Chaillot. As there had been no warning of his approach, the grating still remained closed. He arrived just after the poor girl had fallen from the wooden bench upon the tesselated floor of the cold and cheerless anteroom. Her beautiful form lay apparently lifeless before him. Tears fell profusely from his eyes. He chafed her hands and temples. In endearing terms he entreated her to awake. Gradually she revived. Frankly she related the cause of her departure, and entreated him to permit her to spend the remainder of her saddened life buried in the cloisters of the convent.

The king insisted, with all his authority as a monarch, and with all his persuasive influence as a man, that Louise should return with him to the Louvre. He was inspired with the double passion of love for her, and anger against those who had driven her from his court. Louise, saddened in heart and crushed in spirit, with great reluctance at last yielded to his pleadings. The page was dispatched for a carriage. Seated by the side of the king, Mademoiselle de la Vallière returned to the palace, from which she supposed a few hours before she had departed forever. Louis immediately repaired to the apartment of Madame Henrietta, and so imperiously insisted that Louise should be restored to her place as one of her maids of honor, that his sister-in-law dared not refuse. The influence of Anne of Austria was now nearly at an end. She was dying of slow disease, and, notwithstanding all her efforts to conceal the loathsome malady which was devouring her, she was compelled to spend most of her time in the seclusion of her own chamber.

Louis XIV., in the exercise of absolute power, with all the court bowing before him in the most abject homage, had gradually begun to regard himself almost as a God. He had never recovered from the mortification which he had experienced at the palace of Vaux, in finding a subject living in splendor which outvied that of the crown. He determined to rear a palace of such extraordinary magnificence that no subject, whatever might be his resources, could equal it. For some time he had been looking around for the site of the building, which he had resolved should, like the Pyramids, be a monument of his reign, and excite the wonder and admiration of future ages.

About twelve miles from Paris there was a little village of Versailles, surrounded by an immense forest, whose solemn depths frequently resounded with the baying of the hounds of hunting-parties, as the gayly dressed court

KARTINDO PUBLISHING HOUSE (Kartindo.Com)

swept through the glades.

On one occasion, Louis XIV., in the eagerness of the chase, became separated from most of the rest of the party. Night coming on, he was compelled, and the few companions with him, to take refuge in a windmill, where they remained till morning. The mill was erected upon the highest point of ground. The king caused a small pavilion to be erected there for his accommodation, should he again chance to be overtaken by night or a storm. Pleased with the position, the king ere long removed the pavilion, and ordered his architect, Lemercier, to erect upon the spot an elegant chateau according to his own taste. A landscape gardener was also employed to ornament the grounds. The region soon was embellished with such loveliness as to charm every beholder. It became the favorite rural resort of the king.

The chateau and its grounds soon witnessed a series of festivities, the fame of which resounded through all Europe. Republican America will ponder the fact, which the aristocratic courts of Europe ignored, that these entertainments of boundless extravagance were at the expense of the overtaxed and starving people. That king and courtiers might riot in luxury, the wives and daughters of peasants were harnessed by the side of donkeys to drag the plow.

Early in the spring of 1664, the king, accompanied by his court of six hundred individuals, gentlemen and ladies, with a throng of servants, repaired to Versailles. The personal expenses of all the guests were defrayed by the king with the money which he wrested from the people. With almost magical rapidity, the artificers reared cottages, stages, porticoes, for the exhibition of games, and the display of splendor scarcely equaled in the visions of Oriental romances.

The first entertainment was a tournament. The cavaliers were gorgeously dressed in the most glittering garb of the palmiest days of feudalism, magnificently mounted with wondrous trappings, with their shields and devices, with their attendant pages, equerries, heralds at arms. Among them all the king shone pre-eminent. His dress, and the housings of his charger, embellished with the crown jewels, glittered with a profusion of costly gems which no one else could equal.

The queen, with three hundred ladies of the court, brilliant in beauty, and in the most attractive dress, sat upon a platform, beneath triumphal arches, to view the procession as it passed. The gleaming armor of the cavaliers, their prancing steeds, the waving of silken banners, and the flourish of trumpets, presented a spectacle such as no one present had ever conceived of before.

The tilting did not cease till evening. Suddenly the blaze of four thousand torches illumined the scene with new brilliance. Tables were spread for a banquet, loaded with every delicacy.

"The tables were served by two hundred attendants, habited as dryads, wood deities, and fawns. Behind the tables, which were in the form of a vast crescent, an orchestra arose as if by magic. The tables were illuminated by five hundred girandoles. A gilt balustrade inclosed the whole of the immense area."

KARTINDO PUBLISHING HOUSE (Kartindo.Com)

CHAPTER VI

DEATH IN THE PALACE

1664-1670

Continued festivities.--Molière.--Cost of Versailles.--Lenôtre.--Mansard.--
Large sum squandered.--Magnificent room at Versailles.--Ill feeling toward La
Vallière.--Anne of Austria becomes more ill.--Illness of Maria Theresa.--The
king sick.--Abode of Madame Henrietta.--Sufferings of the queen-mother.--
Death of Philip IV. of Spain.--Increasing ambition of Louis XIV.--Festivities at
St. Cloud.--Dying scene.--Death of the queen-mother.--Funeral ceremonies.--
The Abbey of St. Denis.--Duchess of Vaujours.--Madame de Montespan.--
Daily developments.--Duke de Mazarin--his cynicism.--He is silenced by the
king.--Sale of Dunkirk.--Inconsistencies in the character of Louis.--Treachery
of Montespan.--Sorrows of Louise.--Letters of the Marquis de Montespan.--
Alarm of the marchioness.--Cowardice of the Pope.--Sorrow of the marquis.--
Vexation of Louis.--Petty jealousies.--Employments of the king.--Remarks of
Louis upon court etiquette.--They are unanswerable.--Conquest of Holland
determined on.--Henrietta embassadress to England.--Louise Rénée.--The
bribe.--Constant bickerings.--Alliance between France and England.--
Festivities thereon.--Maria Theresa.--Vivacity of Henrietta.--Henrietta
poisoned.--Intense suffering.--Arrival of the king.--Death scene of Henrietta.--
Suspicion of Louis.--Development of facts.--Statements of M. Pernon.--
Testimony of M. Pernon.--Return of Chevalier de Lorraine.--Marriage of
Monsieur.--Portrait of Charlotte Elizabeth.--Her power of sarcasm.--Sharp
reproof of Madame de Fienne.

The festivities to which we have alluded in the last chapter, the expenses of
which were sufficient almost to exhaust the revenues of a kingdom, lasted
seven days. The prizes awarded to the victors in the lists were very costly and
magnificent. The renowned dramatist Molière accompanied the court on this
occasion, to contribute to its amusement by the exhibition of his mirth-moving
farces on the stage.

It was during these scenes that Louis XIV. selected Versailles as the site of the
stupendous pile of buildings which was to eclipse all other palaces that had
ever been reared on this globe. This magnificent structure, alike the monument

KARTINDO PUBLISHING HOUSE (Kartindo.Com)

of munificence in its appointments, and of infamy in the distress it imposed upon the overtaxed people, eventually swallowed up the sum of one hundred and sixty-six million of francs--thirty-three million dollars. It is to be remembered that at that day money was far more valuable, and far more difficult of acquisition than at the present time.

For seven years an army of workmen was employed on the palace, parks, and gardens. No expense was spared to carry into effect the king's designs. The park and gardens were laid out by the celebrated landscape gardener Lenôtre. The plans for the palace were furnished by the distinguished architect Mansard. Over thirty thousand soldiers were called from their garrisons to assist the swarms of ordinary workmen in digging the vast excavations and constructing the immense terraces. "It is estimated that not less than forty millions sterling-- two hundred million dollars--were exhausted upon the laying out of these vast domains and the erection of this superb chateau. Such was the extraordinary vigor with which the works were pushed, that in 1685, hardly twenty-five years after its commencement, the whole was in readiness to receive its royal occupants. Here the royal family and the court resided until the Revolution of 1789. Every part of the interior as well as the exterior was ornamented with the works of the most eminent masters of the times."[L]

[Footnote L: Bradshaw's Guide through Paris and its Environs.]

The most magnificent room in the palace, called the grand gallery of Louis XIV., was two hundred and forty-two feet long, thirty-five feet broad, and forty-three feet high. The splendors of the court of Louis XIV. may be inferred from the fact that this vast apartment was daily crowded with courtiers. The characteristic vanity of the king is conspicuously developed in that he instituted an order of nobility as a reward for personal services. The one great and only privilege of its members was that they were permitted to wear a blue coat embroidered with gold and silver precisely like that worn by the king, and to follow the king in his hunting-parties and drives.

The position of Mademoiselle de la Vallière was a very painful one. Though the austere queen-mother was so ill in her chamber that she could do but little to harass Louise, Madame Henrietta, who had been constrained to receive her as one of her maids of honor, did every thing in her power to keep her in a state of perpetual anxiety. The courtiers generally were hostile to her, from the partiality with which she was openly regarded by the king. The poor child was alone and desolate in the court, and scarcely knew an hour of joy.

[Illustration: CONVENT OF VAL DE GRACE.]

The queen-mother was rapidly sinking, devoured by a malady which not only caused her extreme bodily suffering, but, from its loathsome character, affected her sensitive nature with the most acute mental pangs. She retired to the convent of Val de Grace, where, with ever-increasing devotion as death drew near, she consecrated herself to works of piety and prayer.

This vast structure is situated upon the left bank of the Seine, and is now in the limits of the city of Paris.

"Anne of Austria had enjoyed the rare privilege, so seldom accorded to her sex, of growing old without in any very eminent degree losing her personal advantages. Her hands and arms, which had always been singularly beautiful, remained smooth and round, and delicately white. Not a wrinkle marred the dignity of her noble forehead. Her eyes, which were remarkably fine, lost neither their brightness nor their expression; and yet for years she had been suffering physical pangs only the more poignant from the resolution with which she concealed them."[M]

[Footnote M: Louis XIV. and the Court of France, vol. ii., p. 145.]

The queen-mother had made the most heroic exertions to assume in public the appearance of health and gayety. None but her physicians were made acquainted with the nature of her malady.

The young queen, Maria Theresa, who appears to have been an amiable, pensive woman, endowed with many quiet virtues, was devotedly attached to the queen-mother. She clung to her and followed her, while virtually abandoned by her royal spouse. She had no heart for those courtly festivities where she saw others with higher fascinations command the admiration and devotion of her husband. The queen was taken very ill with the measles. It speaks well for Louis XIV., and should be recorded to his honor, that he devoted himself to his sick wife, by day and by night, with the most unremitting attention. The disease was malignant in its form, and the king himself was soon stricken down by it. For several days it was feared that he would not live. As he began to recover, he was removed to the palace of St. Cloud. The annexed view represents the rear of the palace. The magnificent saloons in front open upon the city, and from the elevated site of the palace command a splendid view of the region for many leagues around.

[Illustration: THE PALACE OF ST. CLOUD.]

This truly splendid chateau, but a few miles from the Tuileries, had been assigned to Madame Henrietta. Here she resided with her court, and here the king again found himself under the same roof with Mademoiselle de la Vallière.

In the mean time the health of the queen-mother rapidly declined. She was fast sinking into the arms of death. The young queen, Maria Theresa, having recovered, was unwilling to leave her suffering mother-in-law even for an hour.

"The sufferings of Anne of Austria," writes Miss Pardoe, "must indeed have been extreme, when, superadded to the physical agony of which she was so long the victim, her peculiar fastidiousness of scent and touch are remembered. Throughout the whole of her illness she had adopted every measure to conceal, even from herself, the effects of her infirmity. She constantly held in her hand a large fan of Spanish leather, and saturated her linen with the most powerful perfumes. Her sense of contact was so acute and irritable that it was with the utmost difficulty that cambric could be found sufficiently fine for her use. Upon one occasion, when Cardinal Mazarin was jesting with her upon this defect, he told her 'that if she were damned, her eternal punishment would be sleeping in linen sheets.'"

Louis XIV. was too much engrossed with his private pleasures, his buildings, and rapidly multiplying diplomatic intrigues to pay much attention to his dying mother. It was not pleasant to him to contemplate the scenes of suffering in a sick-chamber. The gloom which was gathering around Anne of Austria was somewhat deepened by the intelligence she received of the death of her brother, Philip IV. of Spain. It was another admonition to her that she too must die. Though Philip IV. was a reserved and stately man, allowing himself in but few expressions of tenderness toward his family, Maria Theresa, in her isolation, wept bitterly over her father's death.

The ties of relationship are feeble in courts. Louis XIV. was growing increasingly ambitious of enlarging his domains and aggrandizing his power. The news of the death of the King of Spain was but a source of exultation to him. Though scrupulous in the discharge of the ceremonies of the Church, he was a stranger to any high sense of integrity or honor. In the treaty upon his marriage with Maria Theresa he had agreed to resign every claim to any portion of the Spanish kingdom. The death of Philip IV. left Spain in the hands of a feeble woman. Louis XIV., upon the plea that the five hundred thousand crowns promised as the dower of his wife had not yet been paid, resolved immediately to seize upon the provinces of Flanders and Franche-Comté, which then belonged to the Spanish crown.

Notwithstanding the queen-mother had become so exhausted, from long-continued and agonizing bodily sufferings, that she could not be moved from one bed to another without fainting, still the festivities of the palace continued unintermitted. The moans of the dying queen in the darkened chamber could not be heard amidst the music and the revelry of the Louvre and the Tuileries. On the 5th of January, 1666, Philip, the Duke of Orleans, gave a magnificent ball in the palace of St. Cloud. Louis XIV. was then in deep mourning for his father-in-law. Decorously he wore the mourning dress of violet-colored velvet adopted by the court; he, however, took care so effectually to cover his mourning garments with glittering and costly gems that the color of the material could not be discerned.

While her children were engaged in these revels, the queen-mother passed a sleepless night of terrible suffering. It was apparent to her that her dying hour was near at hand. She was informed by her physician that her life could be continued but a few hours longer. She called for her confessor, and requested every one else to leave the room. What sins she confessed of heart or life are known only to him and to God. Having obtained such absolution as the priest could give, she prepared to partake of the sacrament of the Lord's Supper. Her son Philip, with Madame his wife, were admitted to her chamber, where the king soon joined them. The Archbishop of Auch, accompanied by quite a retinue of ecclesiastics, approached with the holy viaticum. The most scrupulous regard was paid to all the punctilious ceremonials of courtly etiquette.

When the bishop was about to administer the oil of extreme unction, the dying queen requested an attendant very carefully to raise the borders of her cap, lest the oil should touch them, and give them an unpleasant odor. It was one of the most melancholy and impressive of earthly scenes. The king, young, sensitive, and easily overcome by momentary emotion, could not refrain from seeing in that sad spectacle, as in a mirror, his own inevitable lot. He fainted entirely away, and was borne senseless from the apartment.

On the morning of the 7th or 8th of January, 1666, Anne of Austria died. Her will was immediately brought from the cabinet and read. She bequeathed her *heart* to the convent of Val de Grace. It was taken from her body, cased in a costly urn, and conveyed to the convent in a carriage. The Archbishop of Auch seated himself beside the senseless relic, while the Duchess of Montpensier occupied another seat in the coach.

At 7 o'clock of the next evening the remains of the queen left the Louvre for the royal sepulchre at St. Denis. It was a gloomy winter's night. Many torches illumined the path of the procession, exhibiting to the thousands of spectators the solemn pageant of the burial. The ecclesiastics and the monks, in their gorgeous or picturesque robes, the royal sarcophagus, the sombre light of the torches, the royal coaches in funereal drapery, and the wailing requiems, now swelling upon the breeze, and now dying away, blending with the voices of tolling bells, presented one of the most mournful and instructive of earthly spectacles. The queen had passed to that tribunal where no aristocratic privileges are recognized, and where all earthly wealth and rank are disregarded.

The funeral services were prolonged and imposing. It was not until two hours after midnight that the remains were deposited in the vaults of the venerable abbey, the oldest Christian church in France.

[Illustration: INTERIOR OF ST. DENIS.]

The death of the queen-mother does not seem to have produced much effect upon the conduct of her ambitious and pleasure-loving son. He had cruelly betrayed the young and guileless Mademoiselle de la Vallière, and she never ceased to weep over her sad fate. The king, however, conferred upon her the duchy of Vaujours, and the title of Madame. Her beauty began to fade. Younger and happier faces attracted the king. He became more and more arrogant and domineering.

There was at that time rising into notice in this voluptuous court a young lady who was not only magnificently beautiful, but extremely brilliant in her intellectual endowments. She was of illustrious birth, and was lady of the palace to the young queen. She deliberately fixed her affections upon Louis, and resolved to employ all the arts of personal loveliness and the fascinations of wit to win his exclusive favor. She had given her hand, constrained by her family, to the young Marquis de Montespan. She had, however, stated at the time that with her hand she did not give her heart.

The young marquis seems to have been a very worthy man. Disgusted with the folly and the dissipation of the court, he was anxious to withdraw with his beautiful bride to his ample estates in Provence. She, however, entirely devoted to pleasure, and absorbed in her ambitious designs, refused to accompany him, pleading the duty she owed her royal mistress. He went alone. Madame de Montespan was thus relieved of the embarrassment of his presence.

Louis XIV., while apparently immersed in frivolous and guilty pleasures, was developing very considerable ability as a sovereign. It daily became more clearly manifest that he was not a man of pleasure merely; that he had an imperial will, and that he was endowed with unusual administrative energies.

The Duke de Mazarin, a relative and rich heir of the deceased cardinal, and who assumed an austere and cynical character, ventured on one occasion, when displeased with some act of the king, to approach him in the presence of several persons and say,

"Sire, Saint Geneviève appeared to me last night. She is much offended by the conduct of your majesty, and has foretold to me that if you do not reform your morals the greatest misfortunes will fall upon your kingdom."

The whole circle stood aghast at his effrontery. But the king, without exhibiting the slightest emotion, in slow and measured accents, replied,

"And I, Monsieur de Mazarin, have recently had several visions, by which I have been warned that the late cardinal, your uncle, plundered my people, and that it is time to make his heirs disgorge the booty. Remember this, and be persuaded that the very next time you permit yourself to offer me unsolicited advice, I shall act upon the mysterious information I have received."

The duke attempted no reply. Such developments of character effectually warded off all approaches of familiarity.

The fugitive and needy Charles II. had sold to Louis XIV., for about one million of dollars, the important commercial town of Dunkirk, in French Flanders. The king, well aware of the importance of the position, had employed thirty thousand men to fortify the place.

Louis now sent an army of thirty-five thousand men, in the highest state of military discipline, to seize the coveted Spanish provinces of Flanders and

Franche-Comté. At the same time, he sent a reserve of eight thousand troops to Dunkirk. The widowed Queen of Spain, acting as regent for her infant son, could make no effectual resistance. She had but eight thousand troops, in small garrisons, scattered over those provinces. The march of the French army was but as a holiday excursion. Fortress after fortress fell into their hands. Soon the banners of Louis floated proudly over the whole territory. The king displayed his sagacity by granting promotion for services rendered rather than to birth. This inspired the army with great ardor. He also boldly entered the trenches under fire, and exposed himself to the most imminent peril.

The opposite side of the king's character is displayed in the fact that he accompanied the camp with all the ladies of his court, eighteen in number. In each captured city, the king and court, in magnificent banqueting-halls and gorgeous saloons, indulged in the gayest revelry. Amidst the turmoil of the camp, these haughty men and high-born dames surrounded themselves with the magnificence of the Louvre and the Tuileries, and were served with every delicacy from gold and silver plate.

The king, by the advice of his renowned minister of war, Marshal Louvois, placed strong garrisons in the cities he had captured, while the celebrated engineer, M. Vauban, was intrusted with enlarging and strengthening the fortifications. From this victorious campaign Louis XIV. returned to Paris, receiving adulation from the courtiers as if he were more than mortal.

Madame de Montespan accompanied the court on this military pleasure tour. She availed herself of every opportunity to attract the attention of the king and ingratiate herself in his favor. She so far succeeded in exciting the jealousy of the queen against Madame de la Vallière, upon whom she was at the same time lavishing her most tender caresses, that her majesty treated the sensitive and desponding favorite with such rudeness that, with a crushed spirit, she decided to leave the court and retire to Versailles, there to await the conclusion of the campaign. The king, however, interposed to prevent her departure, while at the same time he was daily treating her with more marked neglect, as he turned his attention to the rival, now rapidly gaining the ascendency. The unfortunate Louise was doomed to daily martyrdom. She could not be blind to the fact that the king's love was fast waning. Conscience tortured her, and she wept bitterly. Before her there was opened only the vista of weary years of neglect and remorse.

But the Marchioness of Montespan was mingling for herself a cup of bitterness which she, in her turn, was to drain to its dregs. Her noble husband wrote most imploring letters, beseeching her to return to him with their infant child.

"Come," he wrote in one of his letters, "and take a near view, my dear Athenaïs, of these stupendous Pyrenees, whose every ravine is a landscape, and every valley an Eden. To all these beauties yours alone is wanting. You will be here like Diana, the divinity of these noble forests."

The excuses which the marchioness offered did by no means satisfy her husband. His heart was wounded and his suspicions aroused. At last he was apprised of her manifest endeavors to attract the attention of the king. He wrote severely; informed her of the extent of his knowledge. He threatened to expose her conduct to her own family, and to shut her up in a convent. At the same time, he commanded her to send to him, by the messenger who bore his letter, their little son, that he might not be contaminated by association with so unworthy a mother.

It was too late. The marchioness was involved in such guilty relations with the king that she could not easily be extricated. Still she was much alarmed by the angry letter of her husband. The king perceived her anxiety, and inquired the cause. She placed the letter in his hands. He read it, changing color as he read. He then coolly remarked,

"Our position is a difficult one. It requires much precaution. I will, however, take care that no violence shall be offered you. You had better, however, send him your son. The child is useless here, and perhaps inconvenient. The marquis, deprived of the child, may be driven to acts of severity."

A mother's love was strong in the bosom of the marchioness. She wept aloud, and declared that she would sooner die than part with her son. Her husband soon after came to Paris. He addressed the king in a very firm and reproachful letter, and for three months made earnest applications to the pope for a divorce. But the pope, afraid of offending Louis XIV., turned a deaf ear to his supplications. It was in vain for a noble, however exalted his rank, to contend against the king.

The injured marquis, finding all his efforts vain, returned wifeless and childless to his chateau. Announcing that to him his wife was dead, he assumed the deepest mourning, draped his house and the liveries of his servants in crape, and ordered a funeral service to take place in the parish church. A numerous concourse attended, and all the sad ceremonies of burial were solemnized.

The king was greatly annoyed. The scandal, which spread throughout the kingdom, placed him in a very unenviable position. The marquis would probably have passed the rest of his life in one of the *oubliettes* of the Bastile had he not escaped from France. Madame de Montespan, in her wonderfully frank Memoirs, records all these facts without any apparent consciousness of the infamy to which they consign her memory. She even claims the merit of protecting her injured husband from the dungeon, saying,

"Not being naturally of a bad disposition, I never would allow of his being sent to the Bastile."

There were continual antagonisms arising between Madame de la Vallière and Madame de Montespan. They were both ladies of honor in the household of the queen, who, silent and sad, and ever seeking retirement, endeavored to close her eyes to the guilty scenes transpiring around her. Sin invariably brings sorrow. The king, supremely selfish as he was, must have been a stranger to any peace of mind. He professed full faith in Christianity. Even lost spirits may believe and tremble. The precepts of Jesus were often faithfully proclaimed from the pulpit in his hearing. Remorse must have frequently tortured his soul.

From these domestic tribulations he sought relief in the vigorous prosecution of his plans for national aggrandizement. He plunged into diplomatic intrigues, marshaled armies, built ships, multiplied and enlarged his sea-ports, established colonies, reared magnificent edifices, encouraged letters, and with great sagacity pushed all enterprises which could add to the glory and power of France.

The king had never been on good terms with his brother Philip. Louis was arrogant and domineering. Philip was jealous, and not disposed obsequiously to bow the knee to his imperious brother. The king was unrelenting in the exactions of etiquette. There were three seats used in the presence of royalty: the arm-chair, for members of the royal family; the folded chair, something like a camp-stool, for the highest of the nobility; and the bench, for other dignitaries who were honored with a residence at court. Philip demanded of his brother that his wife, Henrietta, the daughter of Charles I. of England, and the sister of Louis XIII., being of royal blood, should be allowed the privilege of taking an arm-chair in the saloons of the queen. The king made the following remarkable reply:

"That can not be permitted. I beg of you not to persist in such a request. It was not I who established these distinctions. They existed long before you and I were born. It is for your interest that the dignity of the crown should neither be weakened or encroached upon. If from Duke of Orleans you should one day become King of France, I know you well enough to believe that this is a point on which you would be inexorable.

"In the presence of God, you and I are two beings precisely similar to our fellow-men; but in the eyes of men we appear as something extraordinary, superior, greater, and more perfect than others. The day on which the people cast off this respect and this voluntary veneration, by which alone monarchy is upheld, they will see us only their equals, suffering from the same evils, and subject to the same weaknesses as themselves. This once accomplished, all illusion will be over. The laws, no longer sustained by a controlling power, will become black lines upon white paper. Your chair without arms and my arm-chair will be simply two pieces of furniture of equal importance."

To these forcible remarks, indicating deep reflection, the Duke of Orleans, a nobleman rioting in boundless wealth, and enjoying amazing feudal privileges, could make no reply. The coronet of the noble and the crown of the absolute king would both fall to the ground so soon as the masses of the people should escape from the thrall of ignorance and deception. Philip left his brother silenced, yet exasperated. A petty warfare was carried on between them, by which they daily became more alienated from each other.

The king, elated by his easy conquest of Flanders, resolved to seize upon Holland, and then proceed to annex to France the whole of the Low Countries. The Dutch, a maritime people, though powerful at sea, had but a feeble land force. Holland was in alliance with England. The first object of Louis was to dissolve this alliance.

There were two influences, money and beauty, which were omnipotent with the contemptible Charles II. Henrietta, the wife of Philip, was sent as embassadress to the court of her brother. The whole French court escorted her to the coast. The pomp displayed on this occasion surpassed any thing which had heretofore been witnessed in France. The escort consisted of thirty thousand men in the van and the rear of the royal cortège. The most beautiful women of the court accompanied the queen. Maria Theresa, the queen, and Henrietta, occupied the same coach. The ladies of their households followed in their carriages.

The king's two favorites--Madame de la Vallière, whose beauty and power were on the wane, and Madame de Montespan, who was then in the zenith of her triumph--were often invited by the king to take a seat in the royal carriage by the side of the queen and Madame. The most beautiful woman then in the French court was Louise Rénée, subsequently known in English annals as the Duchess of Portsmouth. She was to accompany her royal mistress to the court of Charles II., and had received secret instructions from the king in reference to the influence she was to exert. Louise Rénée was to be the bribe and the motive power to control the king.

Brilliant as was this royal cortège, the journey, to its prominent actors, was a very sad one. The queen, pliant and submissive as she usually was, could not refrain from some expressions of bitterness in being forced to such intimate companionship with her rivals in the king's favor. There were also constant heart-burnings and bickerings, which etiquette could not restrain, between Philip and his spouse Henrietta. *Madame* was going to London as the confidential messenger of the king, and she refused to divulge to her husband the purpose of her visit. Louis XIV. was embarrassed by three ladies, each of whom claimed his exclusive attention, and each of whom was angry if he smiled upon either of the others. In such a party there could be no happiness.

As this gorgeous procession, crowding leagues of the road, swept along, few of the amazed peasants who gazed upon the glittering spectacle could have suspected the misery which was gnawing at the heart of these high-born men and proud dames. Upon arriving at the coast, Henrietta, with her magnificent suite, embarked for England. The negotiation was perfectly successful. The fascinating Louise Rénée immediately made the entire conquest of the king. Her consent to remain a member of his court, and the offer of several millions of money to Charles II., secured his assent to whatever the French king desired. It is said that he the more readily abandoned his alliance with Holland, since he hated the Protestants there, whose religion so severely condemned his worthless character and wretched life. A treaty of alliance was speedily drawn up between Charles II. and Louis XIV.

His Britannic majesty then, with a splendid retinue, accompanied his sister Henrietta to the coast, where she embarked for Calais. The French court met her there with all honors. The return to Paris was slow. At every important town the court tarried for a season of festivities. Henrietta, or *Madame*, as the French invariably entitled her, established her court at St. Cloud. Her husband, Monsieur, was very much irritated against her. Neither of them took any pains to conceal from others their alienation.

Madame was in the ripeness of her rare beauty, and enjoyed great influence in the court. The poor queen, Maria Theresa, was but a cipher. She was heart-crushed, and devoted herself to the education of her children, and to the society of a few Spanish ladies whom she had assembled around her. The king, grateful for the services which Henrietta had rendered him in England, and alike fascinated by her loveliness and her vivacity, was lavishing upon her his constant and most marked attentions, not a little to the chagrin of her irritated and jealous husband.

On the 27th of June, 1669, Henrietta rose at an early hour, and, after some conversation with Madame de Lafayette, to whom she declared she was in admirable health, she attended mass, and then went to the room of her daughter, Mademoiselle d'Orleans. She was in glowing spirits, and enlivened the whole company by her vivacious conversation. After calling for a glass of succory water, which she drank, she dined. The party then repaired to the saloon of *Monsieur*. He was sitting for his portrait. Henrietta, reclining upon a lounge, apparently fell into a doze. Her friends were struck with the haggard and deathly expression which her countenance suddenly assumed, when she sprang up with cries of agony. All were greatly alarmed. Her husband appeared as much so as the rest. She called for another draught of succory water. It was brought to her in an enameled cup from which she was accustomed to drink.

She took the cup in one hand, and then, pressing her hand to her side in a spasm of pain, exclaimed, "I can scarcely breathe. Take me away--take me away! I can support myself no longer." With much difficulty she was led to her chamber by her terrified attendants. There she threw herself upon her bed in convulsions of agony, crying out that she was dying, and praying that her confessor might immediately be sent for. Three physicians were speedily in attendance. Her husband entered her chamber and kneeled at her bedside. She threw her arms around his neck, exclaiming,

"Alas! you have long ceased to love me; but you are unjust, for I have never wronged you." Suddenly she raised herself upon her elbow, and said to those weeping around her, "I have been poisoned by the succory water which I have drank. Probably there has been some mistake. I am sure, however, that I have been poisoned. Unless you wish to see me die, you must immediately administer some antidote."

Her husband did not seem at all agitated by this statement, but directed that some of the succory water should be given to a dog to ascertain its effects. Madame Desbordes, the first *femme de chambre*, who had prepared the beverage, declared that the experiment should be made upon herself. She immediately poured out a glass, and drank it.

Various antidotes for poisons were administered. They created the most deadly sickness, without changing the symptoms or alleviating the pain. It soon became evident that the princess was dying. The livid complexion, glassy eyes, and shrunken nose and lips, showed that some agent of terrific power was consuming her life. A chill perspiration oozed from her forehead, her pulse was imperceptible, and her extremities icy cold.

The king soon arrived, accompanied by the queen. Louis XIV. was greatly affected by the changed appearance and manifestly dying condition of Henrietta. He sat upon one side of the bed and *Monsieur* upon the other, both weeping bitterly. The agony of the princess was dreadful. In most imploring tones she begged that something might be done to mitigate her sufferings. The attendant physicians announced that she was dying. Extreme unction was administered, the crucifix fell from her hand, a convulsive shuddering shook her frame, and Henrietta was dead.

"Only nine hours previously, Henrietta of England had been full of life, and loveliness, and hope, the idol of a court, and the centre of the most brilliant circle in Europe. And now, as the tearful priest arose from his knees, the costly curtains of embroidered velvet were drawn around a cold, pale, motionless, and livid corpse."

A post-mortem examination revealed the presence of poison so virulent in its action that a portion of the stomach was destroyed. Dreadful suspicion rested upon her husband. The king, in a state of intense agitation, summoned his brother to his presence, and demanded that he should confess his share in the murder. Monsieur clasped in his hand the insignia of the Holy Ghost, which he wore about his neck, and took the most solemn oath that he was both directly and indirectly innocent of the death of his wife. Still the circumstantial evidence was so strong against him that he could not escape the terrible suspicion.

Notwithstanding the absolute proof that the death of the princess was caused by poison, still an official statement was soon made out, addressed to the British court, and widely promulgated, in which it was declared that the princess died of a malignant attack of bilious fever. Several physicians were bribed to sign this declaration.

Notwithstanding this statement, the king made vigorous exertions to discover the perpetrators of the crime. The following facts were soon brought to light. The king, some time before, much displeased with the Chevalier de Lorraine, a favorite and adviser of Monsieur, angrily arrested him, and imprisoned him in the Chateau d'If, a strong and renowned fortress on Marguerite Island, opposite Cannes. Here he was treated with great rigor. He was not allowed to correspond, or even to speak with any persons but those on duty within the fortress. *Monsieur* was exceedingly irritated by this despotic act. He ventured loudly to upbraid his brother, and bitterly accused *Madame* of having caused the arrest of his bosom friend, the chevalier.

Circumstances directed the very strong suspicions of the king to M. Pernon, controller of the household of the princess, as being implicated in the murder. The king ordered him to be secretly arrested, and brought by a back staircase to the royal cabinet. Every attendant was dismissed, and his majesty remained alone with the prisoner. Fixing his eyes sternly upon the countenance of M. Pernon, Louis said, "If you reveal every circumstance relative to the death of *Madame*, I promise you full pardon. If you are guilty of the slightest concealment or prevarication, your life shall be the forfeit."

The controller then confessed that the Chevalier de Lorraine had, through the hands of a country gentleman, M. Morel, who was not at all conscious of the nature of the commission he was fulfilling, sent the poison to two confederates at St. Cloud. This package was delivered to the Marquis d'Effiat and Count de Beuvron, intimate friends of the chevalier, and who had no hope that he would be permitted to return to Paris so long as *Madame* lived. The Marquis d'Effiat contrived to enter the closet of the princess, and rubbed the poison on the inside of the enameled cup from which Henrietta was invariably accustomed to drink her favorite beverage.

The king listened intently to this statement, pressed his forehead with his hand, and then inquired, in tones which indicated that he was almost afraid to put the question, "And *Monsieur*--was he aware of this foul plot?"

"No, sire," was the prompt reply. "*Monsieur* can not keep a secret; we did not venture to confide in him."

Louis appeared much relieved. After a moment's pause, he asked, with evident anxiety, "Will you swear to this?"

"On my soul, sire," was the reply.

The king asked no more. Summoning an officer of the household, he said, "Conduct M. Pernon to the gate of the palace, and set him at liberty."

Such events were so common in the courts of feudal despotism in those days of crime, that this atrocious murder seems to have produced but a momentary impression. Poor Henrietta was soon forgotten. The tides of gayety and fashion ebbed and flowed as ever through the saloons of the royal palaces. No one was punished. It would hardly have been decorous for the king to hang men for the murder of the princess, when he had solemnly announced that she had died of a bilious fever. The Chevalier de Lorraine was ere long recalled to court. There he lived in unbridled profligacy, enjoying an annual income of one hundred thousand crowns, till death summoned him to a tribunal where neither wealth nor rank can purchase exemption from crime.

Henrietta, who was but twenty-six years of age at the time of her death, left two daughters, but no son. *Monsieur* soon dried his tears. He sought a new marriage with his rich, renowned cousin, the Duchess of Montpensier. But she declined his offered hand. With inconceivable caprice, she was fixing her affections upon a worthless adventurer, a miserable coxcomb, the Duke de Lauzun, who was then disgracing by his presence the court of the Louvre. This singular freak, an additional evidence that there is no accounting for the vagaries of love, astonished all the courts of Europe. *Monsieur* then turned to the Princess Charlotte Elizabeth of Bavaria. The alliance was one dictated by state policy. *Monsieur* reluctantly assented to it under the moral compulsion of the king. The advent of this most eccentric of women at the French court created general astonishment and almost consternation. She despised etiquette, and dressed in the most *outré* fashion, while she displayed energies of mind and sharpness of tongue which brought all in awe of her. The following is the portrait which this princess, eighteen years of age, has drawn of herself:

"I was born in Heidelberg in 1652. I must necessarily be ugly, for I have no features, small eyes, a short, thick nose, and long, flat lips. Such a combination as this can not produce a physiognomy. I have heavy hanging cheeks and a large face, and nevertheless am short and thick. To sum up all, I am an ugly little object. If I had not a good heart, I should not be bearable any where. To ascertain if my eyes have any expression, it would be necessary to examine them with a microscope. There could not probably be found on earth hands more hideous than mine. The king has often remarked it to me, and made me laugh heartily. Not being able with any conscience to flatter myself that I possessed any thing good looking, I have made up my mind to laugh at my own ugliness. I have found the plan very successful, and frequently discover plenty to laugh at."

Notwithstanding the princess was ready to speak of herself in these terms of ridicule, she was by no means disposed to grant the same privilege to others. She was a woman of keen observation, and was ever ready to resent any offense with the most sarcastic retaliation. She perceived very clearly the sensation which her presence, and the manners which she had very deliberately chosen to adopt, had excited. Madame de Fienne was one of the most brilliant wits of the court. She ventured to make herself and others merry over the oddities of the newly-arrived Duchess of Orleans, in whose court both herself and her husband were pensioners. The duchess took her by the hand, led her aside, and, riveting upon her her unquailing eye, said, in slow and emphatic tones,

"Madame, you are very amiable and very witty. You possess a style of conversation which is endured by the king and by *Monsieur* because they are accustomed to it; but I, who am only a recent arrival at the court, am less familiar with its spirit. I forewarn you that I become incensed when I am made a subject of ridicule. For this reason, I was anxious to give you a slight warning. If you spare me, we shall get on very well together; but if, on the contrary, you treat me as you do others, I shall say nothing to yourself, but I shall complain to your husband, and if he does not correct you, I shall dismiss him."

The hint was sufficient. Neither Madame de Fienne nor any other lady of the court ventured after this to utter a word of witticism on the subject of the Duchess of Orleans.

KARTINDO PUBLISHING HOUSE (Kartindo.Com)

CHAPTER VII

THE WAR IN HOLLAND

1670-1679

Louis's fondness for jewels.--Anecdote.--Superstitions of Louis.--His dread of the towers of St. Denis.--Ambition of Louis.--He abandons St. Germain.-- Severity of Louis to Madame de la Vallière.--A second flitting to Chaillot.-- Night in the convent.--Disappointment.--Return of Louise to the palace.-- Madame de Montespan.--Louis reproved by the clergy.--Power of France.-- Alarm in Holland.--Humble inquiry of the Dutch.--Haughty reply of Louis.-- Body-guard of the king.--Reply of the Dutch merchant.--Forces of William, prince of Orange.--Louis's march unresisted.--The French cross the Rhine.-- Death of the Duke of Longueville.--Passage of the Rhine.--Louis a bigoted Catholic.--Consternation.--Reception of the Dutch deputies.--Terms of Louis XIV.--Heroic conduct of the Dutch.--The dikes pierced.--Naval battle.--Efforts of the Prince of Orange.--Louis returns to Paris.--His extraordinary energy.-- Arch of triumph.--Skill and strategy of Turenne.--Barbarities of Turenne.-- Opinion of Voltaire.--Death of Turenne.--Peace of Nimeguen.--Penitence and anguish of Louise de la Vallière.--Takes leave of her children and the queen.-- Again at the convent.--Faithfulness to duty.--Marriage of the Duchess of Orleans with the King of Spain.--The Countess de Soissons.--Character of the dauphin.--Monseigneur's indifference.--Françoise d'Aubigné.--Her apparent death and recovery.--Françoise a Protestant.--Persecutions in consequence.-- Sufferings of Françoise.--Death of her mother.

Madame de Montespan was now the reigning favorite. The conscience-stricken king could not endure to think of death. He studiedly excluded from observation every thing which could remind him of that doom of mortals. All the badges of mourning were speedily laid aside, and efforts were made to banish from the court the memory of the young and beautiful Princess Henrietta, whose poisoned body was mouldering to dust in the tomb.

The king had a childish fondness for brilliant gems. In his cabinet he had a massive and costly secretary of elaborately carved rosewood. Upon its shelves he had arrayed the crown jewels, which he often handled and examined with the same delight with which a miser counts his gold.

KARTINDO PUBLISHING HOUSE (Kartindo.Com)

Mademoiselle de Montpensier, in her interesting Memoirs, relates the following anecdote, which throws interesting light upon the character of the king at this time. It will be remembered that Louis XIV. was born in one of the palaces at St. Germain, about fifteen miles from Paris. The magnificent terrace on the left bank of the winding Seine commands perhaps as enchanting a view as can be found any where in this world. The domes and towers of Paris appear far away in the north. The wide, luxuriant valley of the Seine, studded with villages and imposing castles, lies spread out in beautiful panorama before the eye. The king had expended between one and two millions of dollars in embellishing the royal residences here. But as the conscience of the king became more sensitive, and repeated deaths forced upon him the conviction that he too must eventually die, St. Germain not only lost all its charms, but became a place obnoxious to him. From the terrace there could be distinctly seen, a few leagues to the east, the tower and spire of St. Denis, the burial-place of the kings of France. To Louis it suddenly became as torturing a sight as to have had his coffin ostentatiously displayed in his banqueting-hall.

When Anne of Austria was lying on her bed of suffering, the king was one day pacing alone the terrace of St. Germain. Dark clouds were drifting through the sky. One of these clouds seemed to gather over the towers of St. Denis. To the excited imagination of the king, the vapor wreathed itself into the form of a hearse, surmounted by the arms of Austria. In a few days the king followed the remains of his mother to the dark vaults of this their last resting-place. Just before the death of the hapless Henrietta, the same gloomy towers appeared to the king in a dream enveloped in flames, and in the midst of the fire there was a skeleton holding in his hand a lady's rich jewelry. But a few days after this the king was constrained to follow the remains of the beautiful Henrietta to this sepulchre. God seems to have sent warning upon warning upon this wicked king. Absorbed in ambitious plans and guilty passions, Louis had but little time or thought to give to his neglected wife or her children. In the same year his two daughters died, and with all the pageantry of royal woe they were also entombed at St. Denis.

[Illustration: ST. DENIS.]

It is not strange that, under these circumstances, the king, to whom the Gospel of Christ was often faithfully preached, and who was living in the most gross violation of the principles of the religion of Jesus, should have recoiled from a view of those towers, which were ever a reminder to him of death and the grave. He could no longer endure the palace at St. Germain. The magnificent panorama of the city, the winding Seine, the flowery meadows, the forest, the villages, and the battlemented chateaux lost all their charms, since the towers of St. Denis would resistlessly arrest his eye, forcing upon his soul reflections from which he instinctively recoiled. He therefore abandoned St. Germain entirely, and determined that the palace he was constructing at Versailles should be so magnificent as to throw every other abode of royalty into the shade.

Madame de la Vallière was daily becoming more wretched. Fully conscious of her sin and shame, deserted by the king, supplanted by a new favorite, and still passionately attached to her royal betrayer, she could not restrain that grief which rapidly marred her beauty. The waning of her charms, and the reproaches of her silent woe, increasingly repelled the king from seeking her society. One day Louis entered the apartment of Louise, and found her weeping bitterly. In cold, reproachful tones, he demanded the cause of her uncontrollable grief. The poor victim, upon the impulse of the moment, gave vent to all the gushing anguish of her soul--her sense of guilt in the sight of God--her misery in view of her ignominious position, and her brokenness of heart in the consciousness that she had lost the love of one for whom she had periled her very soul.

The king listened impatiently, and then haughtily replied, "Let there be an end to this. I love you, and you know it. But I am not to be constrained." He reproached her for her obstinacy in refusing the friendship of her rival, Madame de Montespan, and added the cutting words, "You have needed, as well as Madame de Montespan, the forbearance and countenance of your sex."

Poor Louise was utterly crushed. She had long been thinking of retiring to a convent. Her decision was now formed. She devoted a few sad days to the necessary arrangements, took an agonizing leave, as she supposed forever, of her children, to whom she was tenderly attached, and for whom the king had made ample provision, and, addressing a parting letter to him, entered her carriage, to seek, for a second time, a final retreat in the convent of Chaillot.

It was late in the evening when she entered those gloomy cells where broken hearts find a living burial. To the abbess she said, "I have no longer a home in the palace; may I hope to find one in the cloister?" The abbess received her with true Christian sympathy. After listening with a tearful eye to the recital of her sorrows, she conducted her to the cell in which she was to pass the night.

"She could not pray, although she cast herself upon her knees beside the narrow

KARTINDO PUBLISHING HOUSE (Kartindo.Com)

pallet, and strove to rejoice that she had at length escaped from the trials of a world which had wearied her, and of which she herself was weary. There was no peace, no joy in her rebel heart. She thought of the first days of her happiness; of her children, who on the morrow would ask for her in vain; and then, as memory swept over her throbbing brain, she remembered her former flight to Chaillot, and that it was the king himself who had led her back again into the world. Her brow burned as the question forced itself upon her, Would he do so a second time? would he once more hasten, as he had then done, to rescue her from the living death to which she had consigned herself as an atonement for her past errors?

"But hour after hour went by, and all was silent. Hope died within her. Daylight streamed dimly into the narrow casement of her cell. Soon the measured step of the abbess fell upon her ear as she advanced up the long gallery, striking upon the door of each cell as she approached, and uttering in a solemn voice, 'Let us bless the Lord.' To which appeal each of the sisters replied in turn, 'I give him thanks.'"

The deceptive heart of Louise led her to hope, notwithstanding she had voluntarily sought the cloister, that the king, yearning for her presence, would come himself, as soon as he heard of her departure, and affectionately force her back to the Louvre. Early in the morning she heard the sound of carriage-wheels entering the court-yard of the convent. Her heart throbbed with excitement. Soon she was summoned from her cell to the parlor. Much to her disappointment, the king was not there, but his minister, M. Colbert, presented to her a very affectionate letter from his majesty urging her return. As she hesitated, M. Colbert pleaded earnestly in behalf of his sovereign.

The feeble will of Louise yielded, while yet she blushed at her own weakness. Tears filled her eyes as she took leave of the abbess, grasping her hand, and saying, "This is not a farewell; I shall assuredly return, and perhaps very soon." The king was much moved in receiving her, and, with great apparent cordiality, thanked her for having complied with his entreaties. Even the heart of Madame de Montespan was touched. She received with words of love and sympathy the returned fugitive, whose rivalry she no longer feared, and in whose sad career she perhaps saw mirrored her own future doom.

Madame de Montespan was then in the zenith of her power. The king had assigned her the beautiful chateau of Clagny, but a short distance from Versailles. Here she lived in great splendor, entertaining foreign embassadors, receiving from them costly gifts, and introducing them to her children as if they were really princes of the blood.

Notwithstanding the corruptions of the papal Church, there were in that Church many faithful ministers of Jesus Christ. Some of them, in their preaching, inveighed very severely against the sinful practices in the court. Not only Madame de Montespan, but the king, often knew that they were directly referred to. But the guilty yet sagacious monarch carefully avoided any appropriation of the denunciations to himself. Still, he was so much annoyed that he seriously contemplated urging Madame de Montespan to retire to a convent. He even authorized the venerable Bossuet, then Bishop of Condom, to call upon Madame de Montespan, and suggest in his name that she should withdraw from the court and retire to the seclusion of the cloister. But the haughty favorite, conscious of the power of her charms, and knowing full well that the king had only submitted to the suggestion, peremptorily refused. She judged correctly. The king was well pleased to have her remain.

The preparations which the king was making for the invasion of Holland greatly alarmed the Dutch government. France had become powerful far beyond any other Continental kingdom. The king had the finest army in Europe. Turenne, Condé, Vauban, ranked among the ablest generals and engineers of any age. While Louis XIV. was apparently absorbed in his pleasures, Europe was surprised to see vast trains of artillery and ammunition wagons crowding the roads of his northern provinces. In his previous campaign, Louis had taken Flanders in three months, and Franche-Comté in three weeks. These rapid conquests had alarmed neighboring nations, and Holland, Switzerland, and England had entered into an alliance to resist farther encroachments, should they be attempted.

Louis affected to be very angry that such a feeble state as Holland should have the impudence to think of limiting his conquests. Having, as we have mentioned, detached England from the alliance by bribing with gold and female charms the miserable Charles II., Louis was ready, without any declaration of war, even without any *openly avowed* cause of grievance, to invade Holland, and annex the territory to his realms. The States-General, alarmed in view of the magnitude of the military operations which were being made upon their borders, sent embassadors to the French court humbly to inquire if these preparations were designed against Holland, the ancient and faithful ally of France, and, if so, in what respect Holland had offended.

Louis XIV. haughtily and insolently replied, "I shall make use of my troops as my own dignity renders advisable. I am not responsible for my conduct to any power whatever."

The real ability of the king was shown in the effectual measures he adopted to secure, without the chance of failure, the triumphant execution of his plans. Twenty millions of people had been robbed of their hard earnings to fill his army chests with gold. An army of a hundred and thirty thousand men, in the highest state of discipline, and abundantly supplied with all the munitions of war, were on the march for the northern frontiers of France. These troops were supported by a combined English and French fleet of one hundred and thirty vessels of war. It was the most resistless force, all things considered, Europe had then ever witnessed. We shall not enter into the details of this campaign, which are interesting only to military men. Twelve hundred of the sons of the nobles were organized into a body-guard, ever to surround the king. They were decorated with the most brilliant uniforms, glittering with embroideries of gold and silver, and were magnificently mounted. The terrible bayonet was then, for the first time, attached to the musket. Light pontoons of brass for crossing the rivers were carried on wagons. A celebrated writer, M. Pelisson, accompanied the king, to give a glowing narrative of his achievements.

As there had been no declaration of war and no commencement of hostilities, the king purchased a large amount of military stores even in the states of Holland, which, no one could doubt, he was preparing to invade. A Dutch merchant, being censured by Prince Maurice for entering into a traffic so unpatriotic, replied,

"My lord, if there could be opened to me by sea any advantageous commerce with the infernal regions, I should certainly go there, even at the risk of burning my sails."

Louis made arrangements that money should be liberally expended to bribe the commandants of the Dutch fortresses. To oppose all these moral and physical forces, Holland had but twenty-five thousand soldiers, poorly armed and disciplined. They were under the command of the Prince of Orange, who was in feeble health, and but twenty-two years of age. But this young prince proved to be one of the most extraordinary men of whom history gives any account; yet it was manifestly impossible for him now to arrest the torrent about to invade his courts.

Louis rapidly pushed his troops forward into the unprotected states of Holland which bordered the left banks of the Rhine. His march was unresisted. Liberally

KARTINDO PUBLISHING HOUSE (Kartindo.Com)

he paid for whatever he took, distributed presents to the nobles, and, preparing to cross the river, placed his troops in strong detachments in villages scattered along the banks of the stream. The king himself was at the head of a choice body of thirty thousand troops. Marshal Turenne commanded under him.

The whole country on the left bank of the Rhine was soon in possession of the French, as village after village fell into their hands. The main object of the Prince of Orange was to prevent the French from crossing the river. Louis intended to have crossed by his pontoons, suddenly moving upon some unexpected point. But there came just then a very severe drouth. The water fell so low that there was a portion of the stream which could be nearly forded. It would be necessary to swim the horses but about twenty feet. The current was slow, and the passage could be easily effected. By moving rapidly, the Prince of Orange would not be able to collect at that point sufficient troops seriously to embarrass the operation.

Fifteen thousand horsemen were here sent across, defended by artillery on the banks, and aided by boats of brass. But one man in the French army, the young Duke de Longueville, was killed. He lost his life through inebriation, and its consequent folly and crime. Half crazed with wine, he refused quarter to a Dutch officer who had thrown down his arms and surrendered. Reeling in his saddle, he shot down the officer, exclaiming, "No quarter for these rascals." Some of the Dutch infantry, who were just surrendering, in despair opened fire, and the drunken duke received the death-blow he merited.

This passage of the Rhine was considered a very brilliant achievement, and added much to the military reputation of Louis XIV., though it appears to have been exclusively the feat of the Prince of Condé. The cities of Holland fell in such rapid succession into the power of the French, that scarcely an hour of the day passed in which the king did not receive the news of some conquest. An officer named Mazel sent an aid to Marshal Turenne to say,

"If you will be kind enough to send me fifty horsemen, I shall with them be able to take two or three places."

It was on the 12th of June, 1672, that the passage of the Rhine was effected. On the 20th the French king made his triumphal entrance into the city of Utrecht. The king was a Catholic--a bigoted Catholic. Corrupt as he was in life, regardless as he was in his private conduct of the precepts of Jesus, he was extremely zealous to invest the Catholic Church with power and splendor. It was with him a prominent object to give the Catholic religion the supremacy.

Amsterdam was the capital of the republic. The capture of that city would complete the conquest. Not only the republic would perish, but Holland would, as it were, disappear from the earth, her territory being absorbed in that of France. The consternation in the metropolis was great. The most noble and wealthy families were preparing for a rapid flight to the north. Amsterdam was then the most opulent and influential commercial town in Europe. It contained a population of two hundred thousand sagacious, energetic, thrifty people. As is invariably the case in days of disaster, there were discordant counsels and angry divisions among the bewildered defenders of the imperiled realm. Some were for fiercely pressing the war, others for humbly imploring peace.

At length four deputies were sent to the French camp to intercede for the clemency of the conqueror. They were received with raillery and insult. After contemptuously compelling the deputation several times to come and go without any result, the king at last condescended to present the following as his terms:

He demanded that the States of Holland should surrender to him the whole of the territory on the left bank of the Rhine; that they should place in his hands, to be garrisoned by French troops, the most important forts and fortified towns of the republic; that they should pay him twenty millions of francs, a sum equal to several times that amount at the present day; that the French should be placed in command of all the important entrances to Holland, both by sea and land, and should be exempted from paying any duty upon the goods they should enter; that the Catholic religion should be established every where through the realm; and that every year the republic should send to Louis XIV. an embassador, with a golden medal, upon which there should be impressed the declaration that the republic held all its privileges through the favor of Louis XIV. To these conditions were to be added such as the States-General should be compelled to make with the other allies engaged in the war.

The nations of Europe have been guilty of many outrages, but perhaps it would be difficult to find one more atrocious than this. In reference to the cause of the war, Voltaire very truly remarks, "It is a singular fact, and worthy of record, that of all the enemies, there was not one that could allege any pretext whatever for the war." It was an enterprise very similar to that of the coalition of Louis XII., the Emperor Maximilian, and Spain, who conspired for the overthrow of the Venetian republic simply because that republic was rich and prosperous.

KARTINDO PUBLISHING HOUSE (Kartindo.Com)

These terms, dictated by the insolence of the conqueror, were quite intolerable. They inspired the courage of despair. The resolution was at once formed to perish, if perish they must, with their arms in their hands. The Prince of Orange had always urged the vigorous prosecution of the war. Guided by his energetic counsel, they pierced the dikes, which alone protected their country from the waters of the sea. The flood rushed in through the opened barriers, converting hundreds of leagues of fertile fields into an ocean. The inundation flooded the houses, swept away the roads, destroyed the harvest, drowned the flocks; and yet no one uttered a murmur. Louis XIV., by his infamous demands, had united all hearts in the most determined resistance. Amsterdam appeared like a large fortress rising in the midst of the ocean, surrounded by ships of war, which found depth of water to float where ships had never floated before. The distress was dreadful. It was the briny ocean whose waves were now sweeping over the land. It was so difficult to obtain any fresh water that it was sold for six cents a pint.

Maritime Holland, though weak upon the land, was still powerful on the sea. The united fleet of the allies did not exceed that of the republic. The Dutch Admiral Ruyter, with a hundred vessels of war and fifty fire-ships, repaired to the coasts of England in search of his foes. He met the allied fleet on the 7th of June, 1672, and in the heroic naval battle of Solbaie disabled and dispersed it. This gave Holland the entire supremacy on the sea. Thus suddenly Louis XIV. found himself checked, and no farther progress was possible.

The Prince of Orange gave all his private revenues to the state, and entered into negotiations with other powers, who were already alarmed by the encroachments of the French king. The Emperor of Germany, the Spanish court, and Flanders, entered into an alliance with the heroic prince. He even compelled Charles II. to withdraw from that union with Louis XIV. which was opposed to the interests of England, and into which his court had been reluctantly dragged. Troops from all quarters were hurrying forward for the protection of Holland.

The villainy of Louis XIV. was thwarted. Chagrined at seeing his conquest at an end, but probably with no compunctions of conscience for the vast amount of misery his crime had caused, he left his discomfited army under the command of Turenne and the other generals, and returned to his palaces in France.

The troops which remained in Holland committed outrages which rendered the very name of the French detested. Louis, from the midst of the pomp and

KARTINDO PUBLISHING HOUSE (Kartindo.Com)

pleasure of his palaces, still displayed extraordinary energies. Agents were dispatched to all the courts of Europe with large sums of money for purposes of bribery. By his diplomatic cunning, Hungary was roused against Austria. Gold was lavished upon the King of England to induce him, notwithstanding the opposition of the British Parliament, to continue in alliance with France. Several of the petty states of Germany were bought over. Louis greatly increased his naval force. He soon had forty ships of war afloat, besides a large number of fire-ships.

But Europe had been so alarmed by his encroachments and his menaces that, notwithstanding his efforts at diplomacy and intrigue, he was compelled to abandon his enterprise, and withdraw his troops from the provinces he had overrun.

[Illustration: PORTE ST. DENIS.]

In the early part of his campaign, Louis, flushed with victory and assured of entire success, had commenced building, as a monument of his great achievement, the arch of triumph at the gate of St. Denis. The structure was scarcely completed ere he was compelled to withdraw his troops from Holland, to meet the foes who were crowding upon him from all directions.

Louis XIV. now found nearly all Europe against him. He sent twenty thousand men, under Marshal Turenne, to encounter the forces of the Emperor of Germany. The Prince de Condé was sent with forty thousand troops to assail the redoubtable Prince of Orange. Another strong detachment was dispatched to the frontiers of Spain, to arrest the advance of the Spanish troops. A fleet was also sent, conveying a large land force, to make a diversion by attacking the Spanish sea-ports.

Turenne, in defending the frontiers of the Rhine, acquired reputation which has made his name one of the most renowned in military annals. The emperor sent seventy thousand men against him. Turenne had but twenty thousand to meet them. By wonderful combinations, he defeated and dispersed the whole imperial army. It added not a little to the celebrity of Turenne that he had achieved his victory by following his own judgment, in direct opposition to reiterated orders from the minister of war, given in the name of the king.

Turenne, a merciless warrior, allowed no considerations of humanity to interfere with his military operations. The Palatinate, a country on both sides the Rhine, embracing a territory of about sixteen hundred square miles, and a population of over three hundred thousand, was laid in ashes by his command. It was a beautiful region, very fertile, and covered with villages and opulent cities. The Elector Palatine saw from the towers of his castle at Manheim two cities and twenty-five villages at the same time in flames. This awful destruction was perpetrated upon the defenseless inhabitants, that the armies of the emperor, encountering entire desolation, might be deprived of subsistence. It was nothing to Turenne that thousands of women and children should be cast houseless into the fields to starve.

Alsace, with nearly a million of inhabitants, encountered the same doom. Another province, Lorraine, which covered an area of about ten thousand square miles, and contained a population of one and a half millions, was swept of all its provisions by the cavalry of the French commander. In reference to these military operations, Voltaire writes,

"All the injuries he inflicted seemed to be necessary. Besides, the army of seventy thousand Germans, whom he thus prevented from entering France, would have inflicted much more injury than Turenne inflicted upon Lorraine, Alsace, and the Palatinate."

On the 27th of June, 1675, a cannon ball struck Turenne, and closed in an instant his earthly career. His renown filled Europe. He was a successful warrior, a dissolute man; and few who have ever lived have caused more wide-spread misery than could be charged to his account. Such is not the character which best prepares one to stand before the judgment seat of Christ.

The war continued for two years with somewhat varying fortune, but with unvarying blood and misery. At last peace was made on the 14th of August, 1678--the peace of Nimeguen, as it is styled. Louis XIV. dictated the terms. He was now at the height of his grandeur. He had enlarged his domains by the addition of Franche-Comté, Dunkirk, and half of Flanders. His courtiers worshiped him as a demigod. The French court conferred upon him, with imposing solemnities, the title of *Louis le Grand.* The ambition of Louis was by no means satiated. He availed himself of the short peace which ensued to form plans and gather resources for new conquests.

Let us now return from fields of blood to life in the palace. Madame de la Vallière, upon her return from the convent, soon found herself utterly miserable. She had hoped that reviving affection had been the inducement

KARTINDO PUBLISHING HOUSE (Kartindo.Com)

which led Louis to recall her. Instead of this, his attentions daily diminished. Madame de Montespan had accompanied the king in his brief trip to Holland, and returned with him to Paris. She was all-powerful at court, and seemed to delight, by word and deed, to add to the anguish of her vanquished rival. After a dreary year of wretchedness, Louise could endure no longer a residence in the palace. Her mother, who had been exceedingly distressed in view of the ignominious position occupied by her daughter, entreated her to retire to the Duchy of Vaujours with her children. Her mother promised to accompany her to that quiet yet beautiful retreat. But the spirit of Louise was broken. She longed only to sever herself entirely from the world, and to seek a living burial in the glooms of the cloister. In those days of sorrow, penitence and the spirit of devotion sprang up in her weary heart.

Louise was still young and beautiful. Her passionate love for the king still held strong dominion over her. Grief brought on a long and dangerous illness. For many days her life was in danger. In view of the approaching judgment, where she felt that she soon must stand, the greatness of her transgression harrowed her soul, and increased her desire to spend the rest of her life in works of piety and in prayer. When convalescent, the king consented to her retirement to the Carmelite convent. Like one in a dream, she took leave of her children without a tear. Then, entering the apartment of the queen, she threw herself upon her knees, and with the sobbings of a remorseful and despairing heart implored her pardon for all the sorrow she had caused her. The generous Maria Theresa raised her up, embraced her, and declared her entirely forgiven.

The morning of her departure arrived. The king, who was that day to leave Paris to visit the army in Flanders, attended high mass. Louise also attended. Absorbed in prayer, she did not raise her eyes during the service. She then, pale as death, and leaning upon the arm of her mother, but for whose support she must have fallen, advanced to take leave of the king. The selfish monarch, with a dry eye and a firm voice, bade her adieu, coldly expressing the hope that she would be happy in her retreat. Without the slightest apparent emotion, he saw Louise, with her earthly happiness utterly wrecked, enter her carriage and drive away, to pass the remainder of her joyless years in the gloomy cell of the convent. He then turned and conversed with his companions with as much composure as if nothing unusual had happened.

Louise, upon her arrival at the convent, cast herself upon her knees before the abbess, saying that hitherto she had made so ill a use of her free will that she came to resign it to the abbess forever. For thirty-six years the heart-broken penitent endured the hardships of her convent life--its narrow pallet, its hard fare, its prolonged devotions, its silence, and its rigid fastings. Under the name of Louisa of Mercy she with the most exemplary fidelity performed all her dreary duties, until, in her sixty-sixth year, she fell asleep, and passed away, we trust, to the bosom of that Savior who is ever ready to receive the returning penitent.

The hapless Henrietta, duchess of Orleans, left a very beautiful daughter, Maria Louisa. Her charms of countenance, person, and manners attracted the admiration of the whole court, where she was a universal favorite. She was compelled by the king, as a matter of state policy, to marry Charles II., the young King of Spain, for whom she felt no affection. Bitterly she wept in view of the terrible sacrifice she was compelled to make. But the will of the king was inexorable. Her melancholy marriage was solemnized with much splendor in the great chapel at St. Germain. She then left, with undisguised reluctance, for Madrid. The King of Spain, feeble in body, more feeble in mind, moody and melancholy, was charmed by her youth and beauty. Her mental endowments were such that she soon acquired entire ascendency over him. He became pliant as wax in her hands.

The cabinet at Vienna were alarmed lest Maria Louisa should influence her husband to unite with France against Germany. The Countess de Soissons was sent as a secret agent to the Spanish court. Beautiful and fascinating, she soon became exceedingly intimate with the queen. One day Maria Louisa, oppressed by the heat, expressed regret at the scarcity of milk in Madrid, saying how much she should enjoy a good draught. The countess assured her that she knew where to obtain some of excellent quality, and that, with her majesty's permission, she would have it iced and present it with her own hands. The queen received the cup with a smile, and drank it at once. In half an hour she was taken ill. After a few hours of horrible agony, such as her unhappy mother had previously endured from the same cause, she died. In the confusion, the countess escaped from the capital. She was pursued, but her arrangements for escape had been so skillfully made that she could not be overtaken.

Maria Theresa, the neglected queen of France, had borne six children; but of these, at this period, there was but one surviving son, the dauphin. In his character there appeared a combination of most singular anomalies and contradictions. Though exceedingly impulsive and obstinate in obeying every freak of his fancy, he seemed incapable of any affection, and alike incapable of any hostility, except that which flashed up for the moment.

"The example of his guardians had inspired him with a few amiable qualities,

KARTINDO PUBLISHING HOUSE (Kartindo.Com)

but his natural vices defied eradication. His constitutional tendencies were all evil. His greatest pleasure consisted in annoying those about him. Those who were most conversant with his humor could never guess the temper of his mind. He laughed the loudest and affected the greatest amiability when he was most exasperated, and scowled defiance when he was perfectly unruffled. His only talent was a keen sense of the ridiculous. Nothing escaped him that could be tortured into sarcasm, although no one could have guessed, from his abstracted and careless demeanor, that he was conscious of any thing that was taking place in his presence. His indolence was extreme, and his favorite amusement was lying stretched upon a sofa tapping the points of his shoes with a cane. Never, to the day of his death, had even his most intimate associates heard him express an opinion upon any subject relating to art, literature, or politics."[N]

[Footnote N: Louis XIV. and the Court of France, vol. ii., p. 268.]

Such was the imbecile young man who, by the absurd law of hereditary descent, was the destined heir to the throne of more than twenty millions of people. The king was anxious to obtain for his son a bride whose alliance would strengthen him against his enemies. With that policy alone influencing him, he applied for the hand of the Princess Mary Ann of Bavaria. It so chanced that she was in personal appearance exceedingly unattractive. The king said that, "though she was not handsome, he still hoped that Monseigneur would be able to live happily with her."

The dauphin, or Monseigneur as he was called, seemed to be perfectly indifferent to the whole matter. He at one time inquired if the princess were free from any deformity. Upon being told that she was, he seemed quite contented, and asked no farther questions. In anticipation of the marriage, a lady, Madame de Maintenon, whose name henceforth became inseparably connected with that of Louis XIV., was appointed to the distinguished post of "mistress of the robes" to the dauphiness. We must now introduce this distinguished lady to our readers.

The Marchioness Françoise d'Aubigné was born of a noble Protestant family, in the year 1635, in the prison of Niort. Her mother, with her little boy, had been permitted to join her imprisoned husband in his captivity. Here Françoise was born, amidst scenes of the most extreme poverty and misery. The emaciate mother was unable to afford sustenance to her infant. A sister of Baron d'Aubigné, Madame de Vilette, took Françoise to her home at the Chateau de Marcey, where she passed her infancy. After an imprisonment of four years, the baron was released; but, as he refused to abjure Calvinism, Cardinal Richelieu would not permit him to remain in France. He consequently, with his family, embarked for Martinique. During the passage, Françoise was taken ill and apparently died. As one the crew was about to consign the body to its ocean burial, the grief-stricken mother implored the privilege of one parting embrace. As she pressed the child to her heart, she perceived indications of life. The babe recovered, to occupy a position which filled the world with her renown.

Upon the island of Martinique prosperity smiled upon them.Madame d'Aubigné was a Catholic, though her husband was a Protestant. She at length took ship for France, hoping to save some portion of her husband's sequestered estates, but was unsuccessful. Upon her return to Martinique, she found that Baron d'Aubigné, during her absence, deprived of her restraining influence, had utterly ruined himself by gambling. Overwhelmed by regret and misery,he almost immediately sank into the grave.Madame d'Aubigné and her two children, in the extreme of poverty, returned to France. Madame de Vilette again took the little Françoise to the chateau of Marcey. As her mother was a Catholic, Françoise had been baptized by a Romish priest, and reared in the faith of her mother. The Countess de Neuillant, who was attached to the household of Anne of Austria, was her godmother, and a very intense Catholic; but Madame de Vilette, the sister of the child's father, was a Protestant. The susceptible child was soon led to adopt the faith of her protectress. Catholic zeal was such in those days that Madame de Neuillant obtained an order from the court to remove the little girl from the Protestant family, and to place her under her own guardianship. Here every effort was made to induce Françoise to return to the Catholic faith, but neither threats nor entreaties were of any avail. She remained firm in her Protestant principles.The persecution she endured amounted almost to martyrdom. Madame de Neuillant, in her rage, imposed upon her the most humiliating and onerous domestic services. She was the servant of the servants. She fed the horses. She suffered from cold and hunger. Thus she, who subsequently caused the revocation of the Edict of Nantes, and thus exposed the Protestants to the most dreadful sufferings, was a martyr of the religion of which she later became so terrible a scourge.

The mother, witness the distress her child, succeeded in withdrawing her from Madame de Neuillant, and placing her in a convent. Here the Ursuline nuns won her over to the Catholic faith. Proud of their convert, who was remarkably intelligent and attractive, they kept her for a year. But as neither Madame de Neuillant, from whom she had been removed, nor Madame de Vilette, who dreaded her return to Romanism, would pay her board, they refused to give her any longer a shelter. Françoise left the convent, and joined her mother only in time to see her sink in sorrow to the grave. She was thus left, at fourteen years of age, in utter destitution, dependent upon charity for support.

KARTINDO PUBLISHING HOUSE (Kartindo.Com)

CHAPTER VIII

MADAME DE MAINTENON

1649-1685

Beauty and intelligence of Françoise--Françoise d'Aubigné and the poet Scarron.--Scarron's proposal of marriage.--Marriage of Françoise d'Aubigné.--Becomes a governess.--Elevation of Madame Scarron.--Personal appearance of Madame de Maintenon.--Portrait of Ann of Austria.--The Princess of Tuscany.--Unhappiness of the dauphiness.--Louis's providence for his children.--Mademoiselle de Blois.--Marriage of Mademoiselle de Blois.--The man with the iron mask.--Measures adopted to prevent discovery.--Madame de Montespan and her son.--Mary Angelica Roussille.--Intrigue of Madame de Montespan.--Display of the Duchess de Fontanges.--A quarrel.--Virtuous endeavors of Madame de Maintenon.--Madame de Maintenon's efforts unsuccessful.--Sickness and distress of the Duchess de Fontanges.--Death of the Duchess de Fontanges.--Madame de Montespan rejoices.--Supremacy of Madame de Maintenon.--Père la Chaise.--Remorse of Louis.--Degradation of the people.--Birth of the Duke of Burgoyne.--Louis taken ill.--Dismissal of Madame de Montespan.--Resolves to build a convent.--Her great wealth.--The convent of St. Joseph completed.--The king recovers, and goes to Flanders.--Return to Versailles.--Political ambition of Louis XIV.--Sickness and death of the queen, Maria Theresa.--Tribute to her worth.--Masses.--Versailles.--Heartlessness of the king and of the courtiers.--Accident.--Death of the minister of finance.--Ingratitude.--Remarkable condescension on the part of Louis.--Genoa assailed.--Capture.--The Doge humbled.

The extreme distress and destitution of Françoise touched the heart of Madame de Neuillant. She again took the orphan child under her charge and returned her to school in the convent. Françoise gradually developed remarkable beauty and intelligence. Her quiet, unobtrusive, instinctive tact gave her fascinating power over most who approached her. She often visited the countess, where she attracted much admiration from the fashionable guests who were ever assembled in her saloons. The dissolute courtiers were lavish in their attentions to the highly-endowed child. Established principles of virtue alone saved her from ruin. Misfortune and sorrow had rendered her precocious beyond her years. It was her only and her earnest desire to take the veil, and join the sisters in the convent. But money was needed for that purpose, and she had none.

There was residing very near Madame de Neuillant, a very remarkable man, Paul Scarron. He was born of a good family, and had traveled extensively. Having run through the disgraceful round of fashionable dissipation, he had become crippled by the paralysis of his lower limbs, and was living a literary life in the enjoyment of a competence. He was still young. Imperturbable gayety, wonderful conversational powers, and celebrity as a poet, caused his saloons to be crowded with distinguished and admiring friends. Some one mentioned to him the situation of Françoise d'Aubigné, and her desire to enter the convent. His kindly heart was touched, and, heading a subscription-list, he soon obtained sufficient funds from among his friends to enable her to secure the retreat she desired.

Quite overjoyed, the maiden hastened to the apartments of the poet to express her gratitude. Scarron was astonished when the apparition of a beautiful girl of fifteen, full of life, and with a figure whose symmetric grace the sculptor could with difficulty rival, appeared before him. Her heart was glowing with gratitude which her lips could hardly express, that he was furnishing her with means for a life-long burial in the glooms of the cloister. The poet gazed upon her for a moment quite bewildered, and then said, with one of those beaming smiles which irradiated his pale, intellectual face with rare beauty,

"I must recall my promise; I can not procure you admission into a religious community. You are not fitted for a nun. You can not understand the nature of the sacrifice which you are so eager to make. Will you become my wife? My servants anger and neglect me. I am unable to enforce obedience. Were they under the control of a mistress, they would do their duty. My friends neglect me; I can not pursue them to reproach them for their abandonment. If they saw a pretty woman at the head of my household, they would make my home cheerful. I give you a week to decide."

Françoise returned to the convent bewildered, almost stunned. She was alone in the world, living upon reluctant charity. There was no one to whom she could confidingly look for advice. The future was all dark before her. Scarron, though crippled, was still young, witty, and distinguished as one of the most popular poets of the day. His saloon was the intellectual centre of the capital, where the most distinguished men were wont to meet. At the close of the week Françoise returned an affirmative answer. They were soon married. She found apparently a happy home with her crippled but amiable husband. The brilliant circle in the midst of which she moved strengthened her intellect, enlarged her intelligence,

KARTINDO PUBLISHING HOUSE (Kartindo.Com)

and added to that wonderful ease and gracefulness of manner with which she was by nature endowed.

In the year 1660 Monsieur Scarron died. He had lived expensively, and, as his income was derived from a life annuity which ceased at his death, his wife found herself again in utter destitution. She was then forty-five years of age. Madame de Montespan, who had frequently met her in those brilliant circles, which had been rendered additionally attractive by her personal loveliness and mental charms, persuaded the king to appoint Madame Scarron governess for her children. A residence was accordingly assigned her near the palace of the Luxembourg, where she was installed in her responsible office. She enjoyed a princely residence, horses, a carriage, and a suite of servants. The many attractions of Madame Scarron were not lost upon the king. He often visited her, loved to converse with her, and soon the jealousy of Madame de Montespan was intensely excited by the manifest fondness with which he was regarding the new favorite.

Greatly to the disgust of Madame de Montespan, whose influence was rapidly waning, the king appointed Madame Scarron to the responsible office of *Mistress of the Robes* to the dauphiness, Mary Ann of Bavaria, who was soon to arrive. He also conferred upon her the fine estate of Maintenon, with the title of Marchioness of Maintenon. It was now the turn of Madame de Montespan to experience the same neglect and humiliation through which she had seen, almost exultingly, the unhappy Madame de la Valliére pass.

[Illustration: MADAME DE MAINTENON.]

The haughty favorite had reached her thirty-ninth year. The charms of youth were fast leaving her. Louis had attained his forty-second year. Bitter reproaches often rose between them. The king was weary of her exactions. He made several efforts, but in vain, to induce her to retire to one of the estates which he had conferred upon her. The daily increasing alienation led the king more frequently to seek the soothing society of the calm, gentle, serious Madame de Maintenon. Her fascinations of person and mind won his admiration, while her virtues commanded his respect.

Such was the posture of affairs when preparations were made for the reception of the dauphiness with the utmost magnificence. The costumes of Madame de Maintenon were particularly remarked for their splendor, being covered with jewels and embroidered with gold.

KARTINDO PUBLISHING HOUSE (Kartindo.Com)

"Madame de Maintenon, although in her forty-fifth year, had lost no charm save that of youth, which had been replaced by a stately grace, and a dignified self-possession that rendered it almost impossible to regret the lighter and less finished attractions of buoyancy and display. Her hands and arms were singularly beautiful; her eyes had lost nothing of their fire; her voice was harmoniously modulated, and there was in the whole of her demeanor unstudied ease, which was as far removed from presumption as from servility."[O]

[Footnote O: Louis XIV. and the Court of France, vol. ii., p. 274.]

Madame de Montespan was so annoyed by the honors conferred upon Madame de Maintenon that she was betrayed into saying, "I pity the young foreigner, who can not fail to be eclipsed in every way by her *Mistress of the Robes.*"

Early in the year 1680 Madame de Maintenon and M. Bossuet, bishop of Meaux, who had educated the dauphin, accompanied by a suitable retinue, proceeded to Schelestadt to receive the dauphiness. Here the ceremony of marriage by proxy was to be solemnized. The king and the dauphin proceeded as far as Vitry le Français to receive the bride. She was not beautiful, "but she was," writes Madame de Sévigné, "very graceful; her hands and arms were exquisitely moulded. She had so fine a figure, so admirable a carriage, such handsome teeth, such magnificent hair, and so much amiability of manner, that she was courteous without being insipid, familiar without losing her dignity, and had so charming a deportment that she might be pardoned for not pleasing at first sight."

Louis seemed quite delighted with his new daughter-in-law, and devoted himself much to her entertainment. She was accompanied by her sister, the Princess of Tuscany, who was extremely beautiful. The king, in conversation with Mary Ann, remarked, "You never mentioned to me the fact that the Princess of Tuscany was so singularly lovely." With tact which gave evidence of her self-possession and ready wit, the dauphiness replied, "How can I remember, sire, that my sister monopolized all the beauty of the family, when I, on my part, have monopolized all its happiness."

The young dauphiness had sufficient penetration soon to perceive that the attentions which the king was apparently devoting to her were due mainly to his desire to enjoy the society of the beautiful and agreeable *Mistress of the Robes*. The dauphiness was annoyed. Naturally of a retiring disposition, very fond of books and of music, she soon wearied of the perpetual whirl of fashion and frivolity, and gradually withdrew as much as possible from the society of the court. She imbibed a strong dislike to Madame de Maintenon, which dislike Madame de Montespan did every thing in her power to increase. The dauphiness became very unhappy. She soon found that her husband was a mere cipher, whom she could neither regard with respect nor affection. Louis XIV. allowed the dauphiness to pursue her own course. While ever treating her with the most punctilious politeness, he continued, much to her chagrin, and especially to that of Madame de Montespan, to manifest his admiration for Madame de Maintenon, and constantly to seek her society. Thus the clouds of discontent, jealousy, and bitter hostility shed their gloom throughout the court. There was splendor there, but no happiness.

It was a good trait in the character of the king that he was affectionately attached to *all* of his children. He provided for them sumptuously, and did every thing in his power to provide abundantly for those of dishonorable birth. Royal decrees pronounced them legitimate, and they were honored and courted as princes of the blood.

Mademoiselle de Blois, a daughter of Madame de la Vallière, was one of the most beautiful and highly accomplished women ever seen at the French court. Her mother had transmitted to her all her many virtues and none of her frailties. Tall and slender, her figure was the perfection of grace. A slightly pensive air enhanced the charms of a countenance remarkably lovely, and of a bearing in which were combined the highest attractions of self-respect and courtly breeding. Her voice was music. Her hands and feet were finely modeled. Several foreign princes had solicited her hand. But the king, her father, had invariably declined these offers. He declared that the presence of his daughter was essential to his happiness--that he could not be separated from her.

In 1680 Mademoiselle de Blois was married to the Prince de Conti, nephew of the great Condé. It was as brilliant a marriage as exalted rank, gorgeous dresses, superb diamonds, and courtly etiquette could create. The king could not have honored the nuptials more had he been giving a daughter of the queen to the proudest monarch in Europe. Her princely dowry was the same as would have been conferred on such an occasion. It amounted to five hundred thousand golden crowns. This was the same sum which the Spanish monarchy assigned Maria Theresa upon her marriage with the King of France.

It is difficult to imagine what must have been the emotions of Madame de la Vallière when she heard, in her narrow cell, the details of the brilliant nuptials of her child. Her loving heart must have experienced conflicting sensations of joy and of anguish. Madame de la Vallière had also a son, Count Vermandois. He became exceedingly dissipated, so much so as to excite the severe displeasure of the king. Rumor says that on one occasion he had the audacity to strike the dauphin. The council condemned him to death. Louis XIV., through paternal affection, commuted the punishment to imprisonment for life. The report was spread that he had died of a contagious disease, while he was privately conveyed to the prison of St. Marguerite, and subsequently to the Bastile, his face being ever concealed under an iron mask. Here he died, it is said, on the 19th of November, 1703, after an imprisonment of between thirty and forty years. The true explanation of this great historical mystery will probably now never be ascertained.

The story of the "Man with the Iron Mask" is one of the most remarkable in the annals of the past. Probably no information will ever be obtained upon this subject more full than that which Voltaire has given. He says that a prisoner was sent in great secrecy to the chateau in the island of St. Marguerite; that he was young, tall, and of remarkably graceful figure. His face was concealed by an iron mask, with coils of steel so arranged that he could eat without its removal. Orders were given to kill him instantly if he should announce who he was. He remained at the chateau many years in close imprisonment.

In 1690, M. St. Mars, governor of the prison at St. Marguerite, was transferred to the charge of the Bastile in Paris. The prisoner, ever masked, was taken with him, and was treated on the journey with the highest respect. A well-furnished chamber was provided for him in that immense chateau. The governor himself brought him his food, and stood respectfully like a servile attendant while he ate. The captive was extremely fond of fine linen and lace, and was very attentive to his personal appearance. Upon his death the walls of his chamber were rubbed down and whitewashed. Even the tiles of the floor were removed, lest he might have concealed a note beneath them.

It is very remarkable that, while it can not be doubted that the prisoner was a person of some great importance, no such personage disappeared from Europe at that time. It is a plausible supposition that the king, unwilling to consign his own son to death, sent him to life-long imprisonment; and that the report of his death by a contagious disease was circulated that the mother might be saved the anguish of knowing the dreadful fate of her child. Still there are many difficulties connected with this explanation, and there is none other which has ever satisfied public curiosity.

Madame de Montespan had eight children, who were placed under the care of Madame de Maintenon. Her eldest son, Count de Vixen, died in his eleventh year. Her second son, the Duke de Maine, was a lad of remarkable character and attainments. He loved Madame de Maintenon. He did not love his mother. Unfeelingly he reproached her with his ignoble birth. Madame de Montespan, though still a fine-looking woman, brilliant, witty, and always conspicuous for the splendor of her equipage and her attire, felt every hour embittered by the consciousness that her power over the king had passed away. She regarded the serious, thoughtful Madame de Maintenon as her successful rival, though her social relations with the king were entirely above reproach.

The character of the discarded favorite is developed by the measure she adopted to lure the susceptible and unprincipled monarch from the very agreeable society of Madame de Maintenon. In the department of Provence there was a young lady but eighteen years of age, Mary Angelica Roussille. She was of such wonderful beauty that its fame had reached Paris. Her parents had educated her with the one sole object of rendering her as fascinating as possible. They wished to secure for her the position of a maid of honor to the queen, hoping that by so doing she would attract the favor of the king. Madame de Montespan heard of her. She plotted to bring this young and extraordinary beauty to the court, that, by her personal charms, she might outrival the mental and social attractions of Madame de Maintenon. She described her intended protegé to the king in such enthusiastic strains that his curiosity was roused. She was brought to court. The monarch, satiated by indulgence, oppressed by ennui, ever seeking some new excitement, was at once won by the charms of the beautiful Mary Angelica. She became an acknowledged favorite. He lavished upon her gifts of jewels and of gold, and dignified her with the title of the *Duchesse de Fontanges*. The court blazed again with splendor to greet the new favorite; and, let it not be forgotten, to meet this royal splendor, millions of peasants were consigned to hovels, and life-long penury and want.

There was a constant succession of theatric shows, ballets, and concerts. Mary Angelica was a gay, frivolous, conceited, heartless girl, who recklessly squandered the gold so profusely poured into her lap. The insolent favorite even ventured to treat the queen with disdain, assuming the priority. In the streets she made a truly regal display in a gorgeous carriage drawn by eight cream-colored horses, while the clustering ringlets, the floating plumes, and the truly radiant beauty of the *parvenue* duchess attracted all eyes. If she had ever heard, she refused to heed the warning voice of the prophet, saying, "Know thou that for all these things God will bring thee into judgment."

The scheme of Madame de Montespan had succeeded far more fully than she had expected or desired. The absorption of the king in the new-comer was so entire that the discarded favorite was tortured with new pangs of jealousy and remorse. Implacably she hated the Duchess of Fontanges. With her sharp tongue she mercilessly cut the luxurious beauty, who had intelligence enough to feel the sarcasms keenly, but had no ability to retort. A disgraceful quarrel ensued, in which the most vulgar epithets and the grossest witticisms were bandied between them. The king himself at length found it necessary to interpose. He applied to Madame de Maintenon for counsel and aid. She had quietly attended to her duties, observing all that was passing, but taking no part in these shameful intrigues. Conscious that any attempt to influence Madame de Montespan, hardened as she was in her career, would be futile, she ventured to address herself to the young and inexperienced Duchess de Fontanges. Gently she endeavored to lead her to some conception of the enormity of the life she was leading, and of the indecency of compromising the king and the court by undignified brawls.

The vain and heartless beauty received her counsels with bitter derision and passionate insult, and attributed every annoyance to which, as she averred, she was continually subjected, to the jealous envy of those with whose ambitious views she had interfered; more than hinting that Madame de Maintenon herself was among the number. She was, however, only answered by a placid smile, and instructed to remember that those who sought to share her triumphs and her splendor must be content at the same time to partake her sin. It was a price too heavy to pay even for the smiles of a monarch. In vain did the flushed and furious beauty plead the example of others, higher born and more noble than herself. The calm and unmoved monitress instantly availed herself of this hollow argument to bid her, in her turn, to set an example which the noblest and the best-born might be proud to follow.

"And how can I do this?" was the sullen inquiry.

"By renouncing the society of the king," firmly replied Madame de Maintenon. "Either you love him, or you love him not. If you love him, you should make an effort to save both his honor and your own. If you do not love him, it will cost you no effort to withdraw from the court. In either case you will act wisely and nobly."

"Would not any one believe who heard you," passionately exclaimed the duchess, "that it was as easy to leave a king as to throw off a glove?"[P]

KARTINDO PUBLISHING HOUSE (Kartindo.Com)

[Footnote P: Louis XIV and the Court of France.]

This was the only reply. The mission of Madame de Maintenon had entirely failed. The proud, unblushing beauty, whose effrontery passed all bounds, was greatly enraged against Madame de Maintenon; and when she perceived that the king was again beginning to take refuge in her virtuous society and conversation, she vowed the most signal vengeance.

But the day of retribution soon came--far sooner than could have been expected. The guilty and pampered duchess was taken ill--hopelessly so, with a sickness that destroyed all her beauty. She became sallow, pallid, gaunt, emaciate, haggard. The selfish, heartless king wished to see her no more. He did not conceal his repugnance, and quite forsook her. The humiliation, distress, and abandonment of the guilty duchess was more than she could bear. She begged permission, either sincerely or insincerely, to retire to the convent of Port Royal. Louis, whose crime was far greater than that of his wrecked and ruined victim, was glad to be rid of her. But she was too far gone, in her rapid illness, to be removed. It was soon manifest that her life was drawing near to its close. She begged to see the king once more before she died.

Louis XIV. dreaded every thing which could remind him of that tomb toward which all are hastening, and especially did he recoil from every death-bed scene. The wretched man would not have listened to the plea of the dying girl had not the remonstrances of his confessor constrained him. Thus, reluctantly, he entered the dying chamber. He found Mary Angelica faded, withered, and ghastly--all unlike the radiant beauty whom for a few brief months he had almost worshiped. Egotist as he was, he could not restrain his tears. Her glassy eyes were riveted upon his countenance. Her clammy hand almost convulsively clasped his own. Her livid lips quivered in their last effort as she besought him to pay her debts, and sometimes to remember her. Louis promised all she asked. As she sank back upon her pillow, she gasped out the declaration that she should die happy, as she saw that the king could weep for her. Immediately after she fell into a swoon and died.

The exultation of Madame de Montespan at her death was so indecent and undisguised as to excite the disgust of the king. Her very name became hateful to him. Wicked man as he was, Louis XIV. believed in Christianity, and in its revelations of responsibility at the bar of God. He was shocked, and experienced much remorse in view of this death-bed without repentance. He could not conceal from himself that he was in no inconsiderable degree responsible for the guilt which burdened the soul of the departed. His aversion to Madame de Montespan was increased by the report, then generally circulated, that the duchess had died from poison, administered through her agency. The poor victim of sin and shame was soon forgotten in the grave. The court whirled on in its usual round of frivolous and guilty pleasures, such as Babylon could scarcely have rivaled.

The supremacy of Madame de Maintenon over Louis XIV. was that of a strong mind over a feeble one. The king had many very weak points in his character. He was utterly selfish, and the slave of his vices. Madame de Maintenon, with much address, strove to recall him to a better life. In these efforts she was much aided by the king's confessor, Père la Chaise. This truly good man reminded the king that he had already passed the fortieth year of his age, that his youth had gone forever, that he would soon enter upon the evening of his days, and that, as yet, he had done nothing to secure his eternal salvation. He had already received many warnings as he had followed one after another to the grave. The king was naturally thoughtful, and perhaps even religiously inclined. Not a few events had already occurred calculated to harrow his soul with remorse. He had seen his mother die, one of the saddest of deaths. He had seen his sister Henrietta, his brother's bride, whom he had loved with more than a brother's love, writhing in death's agonies, the victim of poison. He had followed several of his children to the grave. Madame de la Vallière, whom he had loved as ardently as he was capable of loving any one, now a ruined, heart-broken victim of his selfishness and sin, was consigned to living burial in the glooms of the cloister. He could not banish from his mind the dreadful scenes of the death of the Duchess of Fontanges.

Just at this time the dauphiness gave birth to a son. This advent of an heir to the throne caused universal rejoicing throughout the court and the nation. It is melancholy to reflect that the people, crushed and impoverished as they were by the most atrocious despotism, were so unintelligent that they regarded their oppressors with something of the idolatrous homage with which the heathen bow before their hideous gods.

The king himself, at times, manifested a kind of tender interest in the people, who were so mercilessly robbed to maintain the splendor of his court and the grandeur of his armies. Upon the birth of the young prince, who received the title of the Duke of Burgoyne, the populace of Paris crowded to Versailles with their rude congratulations. Every avenue was thronged with the immense multitude. They even flooded the palace and poured into the saloons. The king, whose heart was softened by the birth of a grandson to whom the crown might be transmitted, received all very graciously.

The birth of an heir to the crown added much to the personal importance of the dauphiness. But, neglected by her husband and annoyed by the scenes transpiring around her, she was a very unhappy woman. No efforts on the part of the court could draw her from the silence and gloom of her retirement. Madame de Maintenon and the king's confessor, Père la Chaise, were co-operating in the endeavor to lure the king from his life of guilty indulgence into the paths of virtue. Fortunately, at this time the monarch was attacked by severe and painful illness. Death was to him truly the king of terrors. He was easily influenced to withdraw from his criminal relations with one whom he had for some time been regarding with repugnance. Madame de Maintenon was deputed to inform Madame de Montespan of the king's determination never again to regard her in any other light than that of a friend.

It was a very painful and embarrassing commission for Madame de Maintenon to fulfill. But the will of the king was law. She discharged the duty with great delicacy and kindness. Deeply mortified as was the discarded favorite, she was not entirely unprepared for the announcement. She had for some time been painfully aware of her waning influence, and had been preparing for herself a retreat where she could still enjoy opulence, rank, and power.

In pursuit of this object, she had determined to erect and endow a convent. The sisterhood, appointed by her and entirely dependent upon her liberality, would treat her with the deference due to a queen. The king had lavished such enormous sums upon her that she had large wealth at her disposal. She had already selected a spot for the convent in the Faubourg St. Germain, and had commenced rearing the edifice. It so happened that the corner-stone was laid at the very moment in which the unhappy Duchess de Fontanges was breathing her last. Madame de Montespan had no idea of taking the veil herself. The glooms of the cloister had for her no attractions. Her only object was to rear a miniature kingdom, where she, having lost the potent charms of youth and beauty, could still enjoy an undisputed reign.

The marchioness already owned a dwelling, luxuriously furnished, which the king had presented her, in the Rue St. Andre des Arcs. Her wealth was so great that, in addition to the convent, she also planned erecting for herself a magnificent hotel, in imitation of the palace of the Tuileries. The estimated expense was equal to the sum of one million five hundred thousand dollars at the present day.

The workmen upon the convent were urged to the most energetic labor, and the building was soon completed. The marchioness gave it the name of St. Joseph.

One room was sumptuously furnished for her private accommodation. She appointed the abbess. The great bell of the convent was to ring twenty minutes whenever she visited the sisterhood. As the founder of the community, she was to receive the honors of the incense at high mass and vespers. The marchioness richly enjoyed this adulation, and was a frequent visitor at the convent.

The king, having recovered from his illness, decided upon a journey to Flanders. Oppressed with ennui, he sought amusement for himself and his court. He wished also to impress his neighbors by an exhibition of his splendor and power. The queen, with the dauphin and dauphiness, attended by their several suites, accompanied him on this expedition. Madame de Montespan was excessively chagrined in finding her name omitted in the list of those who were to make up the party. But the name of Madame de Maintenon headed the list of the attendants of the princess.

The gorgeous procession, charioted in the highest appliances of regal splendor, swept along through cities and villages, every where received with triumphal arches, the ringing of bells, the explosions of artillery, and the blaze of illuminations till the sea-port of Dunkirk was reached. Here there was a sham-fight between two frigates. It was a serene and lovely day. The members of the royal suite, from the deck of a bark sumptuously prepared for their accommodation, witnessed with much delight the novel spectacle. At the close, the king repaired to one of the men-of-war, upon whose deck a lofty throne was erected, draped with a costly awning. Here the splendor-loving monarch, surrounded by that ceremonial and pageantry which were so dear to him, received the congratulations of the dignitaries of his own and other lands upon his recent recovery from illness. At the end of a month the party returned to Versailles.

Devoted as Louis XIV. was to his own selfish gratification, he was fully aware of the dependence of that gratification upon the aggrandizement of the realm, which he regarded as his private property. Upon this tour of pleasure he invested the city of Luxembourg with an army of thirty thousand men, and took it after a siege of eight days. He then overrun the Electorate of Treves, demolished all its fine fortifications, and by the energies of pillage, fire, and ruin, rendered it impossible for the territory hereafter to render any opposition to his arms. The destructive genius of Louvois had suggested that these unnecessary spoliations would tend to increase the authority of his royal master by inspiring a greater terror of his power.

Soon after this, the queen, Maria Theresa, was suddenly taken sick. Her indisposition, at first slight, rapidly increased in severity, and an abscess developed itself under her arm. The pain became excruciating. Her physician opened a vein and administered an emetic at 11 o'clock in the morning. It was a fatal prescription. At 3 o'clock in the afternoon she died. As this unhappy queen, so gentle, so loving, so forgiving, was sinking away in death, she still, with woman's deathless love, cherished tenderly in her heart the memory of the king. Just as she was breathing her last, she drew from her finger a superb ring, which she presented to Madame de Maintenon saying,

"Adieu, my very dear marchioness. To you I confide the happiness of the king."

Maria Theresa was one of the most lovely of women. Her conduct was ever irreproachable. Amiable, unselfish, warm-hearted, from the time of her marriage she devoted herself to the promotion of the happiness of her husband. His neglect and unfaithfulness caused her, in secret, to shed many tears. Naturally diffident, and rendered timid by his undisguised indifference, she trembled whenever the king approached her. A casual smile from him filled her with delight. The king could not be insensible to her many virtues. Perhaps remorse was mingled with the emotions which compelled him to weep bitterly over her death. As he gazed upon her lifeless remains, he exclaimed,

"Kind and forbearing friend, this is the first sorrow that you have caused me throughout twenty years."

[Illustration: PALACE OF VERSAILLES.]

The royal corpse lay in state at Versailles for ten days. During this time perpetual masses were performed for the soul of the departed from 7 o'clock in the morning until dark. The king had reared the gorgeous palace of Versailles that he might not be annoyed, in his Babylonian revelry, by the sight of the towers of St. Denis. But God did not allow the guilty monarch to forget that kings as well as peasants were doomed to die. The king was compelled to accompany the remains of Maria Theresa from the sumptuous palace, where she had found so splendid and so unhappy a home, to the gloomy vaults of the abbey, where, in darkness and silence, those remains were to moulder to dust.

The queen was forgotten even before she was buried. The gay courtiers, anxious to banish as speedily as possible from their minds all thoughts of death and judgment, sought, in songs, and mirth, and wine, to bury even the grave in oblivion. The funeral car was decorated with the most imposing emblems of mourning. A numerous train of carriages followed, filled with the great officers of the crown and with the ladies of the royal household. The procession was escorted by a brilliant and numerous body of mounted troops.

"But nothing could exceed the indecency with which the journey was performed. From all the carriages issued the sounds of heartless jest and still more heartless laughter. The troops had no sooner reached the plain of St. Denis than they dispersed in every direction, some galloping right and left, and others firing at the birds that were flying over their heads."[Q]

[Footnote Q: Memoirs of Mademoiselle de Montpensier.]

The king, on the day of the funeral, in the insane endeavor to obliterate from his mind thoughts of death and burial, ordered out the hounds and plunged into the excitement of the chase. His horse pitched the monarch over his head into a ditch of stagnant water, dislocating one of his shoulders.

About this time, Jean Baptiste Colbert, the king's minister of finance, and probably the most extraordinary man of the age, died, worn out with toil, anxiety, and grief. Few men have ever passed through this world leaving behind them such solid results of their labors. As minister of finance, he furnished the king with all the money he needed for his expensive wars and luxurious indulgence. As superintendent of buildings, arts, and manufactures, he enlarged the Tuileries, completed the gorgeous palace of Versailles, reared the magnificent edifices of the Invalides, Vincennes, and Marly, and founded the Gobelins. These and many other works of a similar nature he performed, though constantly struggling against the jealousy and intrigues of powerful opponents.

The king seldom, if ever, manifested any gratitude to those who served him. Colbert, in the 64th year of his age, exhausted by incessant labor, and harassed by innumerable annoyances, was on a dying bed. Sad reflections seemed to overwhelm him. Not a gleam of joy lighted up his fading eye. The heavy taxes he had imposed upon the people rendered him unpopular. He could not be insensible to imprecations which threatened to break up his funeral and to drag his remains ignominiously through the streets. The king condescended, as his only act of courtesy, to send a messenger to ask tidings of the condition of his minister. As the messenger approached the bed, the dying sufferer turned away his face, saying,

"I will not hear that man spoken of again. If I had done for God what I have done for him, I should have been saved ten times over. Now I know not what may be my fate."

The day after his death, without any marks of honor, his remains were conveyed, in an ordinary hearse, to the church of St. Eustache. A few of the police alone followed the coffin.

Genoa had offended the king by selling powder to the Algerines, and some ships to Spain. Louis seized, by secret warrant, *lettre de cachet*, the Genoese embassador, and plunged him into one of the dungeons of the Bastile. He then sent a fleet of over fifty vessels of war to chastise, with terrible severity, those who had offended him. The ships sailed from Toulon on the 6th of May, 1684, and entered the harbor of Genoa on the 19th. Immediately there was opened upon the city a terrific fire. In a few hours fourteen thousand bombs were hurled into its dwellings and its streets. A large portion of those marble edifices, which had given the city the name of *Genoa the Superb*, were crumbled to powder. Fourteen thousand soldiers were then disembarked. They advanced through the suburbs, burning the buildings before them. The whole city was threatened with total destruction. The authorities, in terror, sent to the conqueror imploring his clemency. The haughty King of France demanded that the Doge of Genoa, with four of his principal ministers, should repair to the palace of Versailles and humbly implore his pardon. The doge, utterly powerless, was compelled to submit to the humiliating terms.

CHAPTER IX

THE REVOCATION OF THE EDICT OF NANTES

1680-1686

Character of Madame de Maintenon.--Depression of the dauphiness.--Père la Chaise.--The Edict of Nantes.--The Catholic clergy indignant.--Ravaillac.--Confirmation of the Edict of Nantes.--La Rochelle.--Sufferings of the Huguenots.--Policy of Louis.--Influence of Madame de Maintenon.--Religious zeal of the king.--False-hearted.--Persecution of the Protestants.--Severe measures to force proselytism.--The *dragonnades*.--Moral suasion of the dragoons.--Brutality of the soldiery.--Enactments of intolerance.--Zeal of the king.--The revocation of the Edict of Nantes.--Severe enactments against the Protestants.--Flight of the Protestants.--Numbers of the emigrants.--Scenes of suffering.--Louis alarmed.--Historical accounts of the emigration.--Multiplied outrages.--Reactions.--Secret assemblies.--Rage of the Jesuits.--New measures of the court.--Remonstrances of honorable Catholics.--Intrigues of the king.--Madame de Montespan to be removed.--Banishment of Madame de Montespan.--Parterre of Versailles.--A successful mission.--Egotism and heartlessness of the king.--Singular interview.--The king defends Madame de Maintenon's character.--Scene of frenzy and despair.--Madame de Maintenon and Madame de Montespan.

It is the undisputed testimony of all the contemporaries of Madame de Maintenon that she possessed a character of rare excellence. Her personal attractions, sound judgment, instinctive delicacy of perception, and conversational brilliance, gave her a certain supremacy wherever she appeared. The fidelity with which she fulfilled her duties, her high religious principles, and the bold, yet tender remonstrances with which she endeavored to reclaim the king from his unworthy life, excited first his astonishment, and then his profound admiration.

Every day the king, at three o'clock, proceeded to the apartments of Madame de Maintenon, and, taking a seat in an arm-chair, sat in a reclining posture, sometimes silently watching the progress of her tapestry-work, and again engaged in quiet conversation. Occasionally some of Racine's tragedies were read. The king took a listless pleasure in drawing out Madame de Maintenon to remark upon the merits or defects of the production.

"In truth, a weariness of existence was rapidly growing upon Louis XIV. He had outlived his loves, his griefs, and almost his ambition. All he wanted was repose. And this he found in the society of an accomplished, judicious, and unassuming woman, who, although she occasionally transacted business in her presence with Louvois, never presumed to proffer an opinion save when he appealed to her judgment, and even then tendered it with reluctance and reserve."[R]

[Footnote R: Louis XIV. and the Court of France, by Miss Pardoe, vol. ii., p. 339.]

Upon the death of the queen the dauphiness was raised to the first rank at court. Still she was gloomy and reserved. No allurements could draw her from her retirement. Madame de Maintenon was a very decided Roman Catholic, and was very much influenced by the king's confessor, Père la Chaise, who seems to have been a man of integrity and of conscientiousness, though fanatically devoted to what he deemed to be the interests of the Church. In former reigns the Protestants had endured from the Catholics the most dreadful persecutions. After scenes of woe, the recital of which causes the blood to curdle in one's veins, Henry IV., the grandfather of Louis XIV., feeling the need of the support of the Protestants to protect the kingdom from the perils by which it was surrounded, and having himself been educated a Protestant, granted the Protestants the world-renowned Edict of Nantes.

By this edict, which took its name from the place in which it was published, and which was issued in April, 1598, certain privileges were granted to the Protestants, which, in that dark age, were regarded as extraordinarily liberal.

Protestants were allowed liberty of conscience; that is, they were not to be punished for their religious faith. In certain designated places they were permitted to hold public worship. The highest lords of the Protestant faith could celebrate divine service in their castles. Nobles of the second rank could have private worship, provided but thirty persons attended. Protestants were declared to be eligible to offices of state, their children were to be admitted to the public schools, their sick to the hospitals, and their poor to the public charities. In certain places they could publish books; they were allowed four academies for scientific and theological instruction, and were permitted to convoke synods for Church discipline.

The Catholic clergy were very indignant in view of these concessions. Pope Clement VIII. declared that the ordinance which permitted liberty of conscience to every one was the most execrable which was ever made.[S]

[Footnote S: History of the Protestants of France, by Professor G. de Félice, p. 275.]

There were then seven hundred and sixty churches in France of the Protestant communion. No such church was allowed in Paris. Protestants from the city, rich and poor, were compelled to repair, for public worship, to the little village of Ablon, fifteen miles from the city. The Edict of Nantes probably cost Henry IV. his life. The assassin Ravaillac, who plunged his dagger twice into the bosom of the king, said, in his examination,

"I killed the king because, in making war upon the pope, he made war upon God, since the pope is God."

The Protestants were thrown into the utmost consternation by the death of Henry IV. They apprehended the immediate repeal of the edict, and a renewal of the massacre of St. Bartholomew's Day. But the regent, Mary de Medici, and the court immediately issued a decree confirming the ordinance. Louis XIII. was then a child but eight and a half years of age. As he came into power, he was urged by the Jesuits to exterminate the Protestants. But they were too powerful to be wantonly assailed. They held two hundred fortified places. Many of the highest lords were among their leaders. Their soldiers were renowned for valor, and their churches numbered four hundred thousand men capable of bearing arms. It was not deemed safe to rouse such a people to the energies of despair. Still, during the reign of Louis XIII., there were many bloody conflicts between the royal troops and the Protestants.

In this religious war, the Protestants, or Huguenots, as they were then called, defended themselves so valiantly, that the king felt constrained, in October, 1622, to relinquish his attempt to subjugate the Protestants by force of arms, and to confirm the Edict of Nantes. The sword was scarcely sheathed ere it was drawn again. All over France the Catholics and Protestants faced each other upon fields of blood. The battle raged for seven years with every conceivable concomitant of cruelty and horror. The eyes of all Europe were directed to the siege of La Rochelle, in 1627, where the Huguenots made their most decisive stand. All that human nature could suffer was endured. When two thirds of the population of the city had perished, and the streets and dwellings were encumbered with the unburied dead, and the remaining soldiers, reduced to skeletons, could no longer lift their weapons, the city surrendered on the 28th of October, 1628.

By this war and the fall of La Rochelle, the Protestants were hopelessly weakened. Though they were deprived of many of their privileges, and were greatly diminished in numbers and influence, still the general provisions of the Edict of Nantes were not repealed.

In the year 1662, Louis XIV., then upon the throne, in recognition of some support which he had received from the Protestants, issued a decree in which he said,

"Inasmuch as our subjects of the pretended Reformed religion have given us proofs of their affection and fidelity, be it known that, for these reasons, they shall be supported and guarded, as in fact we do support and guard them, in the full enjoyment of the Edict of Nantes."

The king had even appointed, the year before, two commissaries, the one a Catholic, the other a Protestant, to visit every province, and see that the requisitions of the Edict of Nantes were faithfully observed. This seemed very fair. But, in appointing these commissioners, a Catholic was always appointed who was a high dignitary of the state, a man of wealth and rank, distinguished for his devotion to the interests of the Catholic Church. On the other hand, the Protestant was always some poor country gentleman, timid and irresolute, and often one who had been secretly sold to the court to betray his duties.

The Protestants had hoped much from the influence of Madame de Maintenon over the king, as she was the granddaughter of Agrippa d'Aubigné, one of the most illustrious defenders of the Calvinistic faith, and as she herself had been a Protestant until she had attained the age of sixteen years.

But the king was fanatically Catholic, hoping, in some measure, to atone for his sins by his supreme devotion to the interests of the Church. Madame de Maintenon found it necessary, in promotion of her ambitious plans, to do all in her power to conceal her Protestant origin. She was fully aware of the king's great dislike to the Protestants, and of the necessity of cordially co-operating with him in these views. Still she could not refrain from manifesting some compassion at times for the sufferings of the friends of her earlier years.

Louis XIV., while assuring the Protestant powers of Europe that he would continue to respect the Edict of Nantes, commenced issuing a series of ordinances in direct opposition to that contract. First he excluded Protestants from all public offices whatever. A Protestant could not be employed as a physician, lawyer, apothecary, bookseller, printer, or even as a nurse. This decree was issued in 1680. In some portions of the kingdom the Protestants composed nearly the entire population. Here it was impossible to enforce the atrocious decree. In other places it led to riots and bloodshed.

This ordinance was followed by one forbidding marriages between Catholics and Protestants. Catholic servants were forbidden to serve in Protestant families, and Protestant servants could not be employed by Catholics.

Rapidly blow followed blow. On the 17th of June, 1680, the king issued the following ordinance: "We wish that our subjects of the pretended Reformed religion, both male and female, having attained the age of seven years, may, and it is hereby made lawful for them to embrace the Catholic Apostolic and Roman religion, and that to this effect they be allowed to abjure the pretended Reformed religion, without their fathers and mothers and other kinsmen being allowed to offer them the least hinderance, under any pretext whatever."

The effect of this law was terrible. Any malignant person, even a servant, could go into a court of justice and testify that a certain child had made the sign of the cross, or kissed an image of the Virgin, or had expressed a desire to enter the Catholic Church, and that child was immediately taken from its parents, shut up in a convent, and the parents were compelled to pay the expenses of its education. Even Madame de Maintenon availed herself of this law in wresting from her relative, the Marquis de Vilette, his children.

A decree was then issued that all Protestants who should become Catholics might defer the payment of their debts for three years, and for two years be exempt from taxation, and from the burden of having soldiers quartered upon them. To save the treasury from loss, a double burden of taxation and a double quartering of soldiers was imposed upon those Protestants who refused to abjure their faith.

If any Protestant was sick, officers were appointed whose duty it was to visit

KARTINDO PUBLISHING HOUSE (Kartindo.Com)

the sick-bed, and strive to convert the sufferer to the Catholic faith. Any physician who should neglect to give notice of such sickness was punished by a severe fine. The pastors were forbidden to make any allusions whatever in their sermons to these decrees of the court. Following this decree came the announcement that if any convert from Catholicism should be received into a Protestant Church, his property should be confiscated, he should be banished, and the privilege of public worship should no longer be enjoyed by that Church. Under this law several church edifices were utterly demolished.

One of the severest measures adopted against the Protestants was quartering brutal and ferocious soldiers in their families. In March, 1681, Louvois wrote to the governor of Poitou that he intended to send a regiment of cavalry into that province.

"His majesty," he said, "has learned with much satisfaction the great number of persons who are becoming converts in your province. He desires that you continue to give great care to this matter. He thinks it best that the chief part of the cavalry and officers should be lodged in the houses of the Protestants. If, after a just distribution, the Calvinists would have to provide for ten soldiers, you can make them take twenty."

The governor, Marillac, lodged from four to ten dragoons in the house of every Protestant. The soldiers were directed not to kill the people with whom they lodged, but to do every thing in their power to constrain them to abjure Protestantism. Thus originated that system of *dragonnades* which has left an indelible stain upon the character of Louis XIV., and the recital of which has inspired every reader with horror.

"The cavalry attached crosses to the muzzles of their muskets to force the Protestants to kiss them. When any one resisted, they thrust these crosses against the face and breasts of the unfortunate people. They spared children no more than persons advanced in years. Without compassion for their age, they fell upon them with blows, and beat them with the flat side of their swords and the butt of their muskets. They did this so cruelly that some were crippled for life."[T]

[Footnote T: Histoire de l'Edit de Nantes, t. iv., p. 479.]

It does not reflect credit upon Madame de Maintenon that she was eager to enrich her friends from the spoils of these persecuted Christians. Her brother was to receive a present of one hundred and eight thousand francs ($21,600). This sum was then three or four times as much as the same amount of money now.

A law was now passed prohibiting the Protestants from leaving the kingdom, and condemning to perpetual imprisonment in the galleys all who should attempt to escape. France was ransacked to find every book written in support of Protestantism, that it might be burned. A representation having been made to the king of the sufferings of more than two millions of Protestant Frenchmen, he sternly replied,

"To bring back all my subjects to Catholic unity, I would readily, with one hand, cut off the other."

In some places the Protestants were goaded to an appeal to arms. With the most merciless butchery they were cut down, their houses razed, while some were put to death by lingering torture. In September, 1685, Louvois wrote,

"Sixty thousand conversions have taken place in the district of Bordeaux, and twenty thousand in that of Montauban. The rapidity with which they go on is such that, before the end of the month, there will not remain ten thousand Protestants in all the district of Bordeaux, where there were one hundred and fifty thousand the 15th of last month."

The Duke of Noailles wrote to Louvois, "The number of Protestants in the district of Nismes is about one hundred and forty thousand. I believe that at the end of the month there will be none left."

On the 18th of October, 1685, the king, acceding to the wishes of his confessor and other high dignitaries of the Church, signed the *Revocation of the Edict of Nantes*.

In the preamble to this fatal act, it was stated,

"We see now, with the just acknowledgment we owe to God, that our measures have secured the end which we ourselves proposed, since the better and greater part of our subjects of the pretended Reformed religion have embraced the Catholic faith, and the maintenance of the Edict of Nantes remains therefore superfluous."

In this act of revocation it was declared that the exercise of the Protestant worship should nowhere be tolerated in the realm of France. All Protestant pastors were ordered to leave the kingdom within fifteen days, under pain of being sent to the galleys. Those Protestant ministers who would abjure their faith and return to Catholicism were promised a salary one third more than they had previously enjoyed. Parents were forbidden to instruct their children in the Protestant religion. Every child in the kingdom was to be baptized and educated by a Catholic priest. All Protestants who had left France were ordered to return within four months, under penalty of the confiscation of their possessions. Any Protestant layman, man or woman, who should attempt to emigrate, incurred the penalty of imprisonment for life.

This infamous ordinance caused an amount of misery which can never be gauged, and inflicted upon the prosperity of France the most terrible blow it had ever received. Hundreds of thousands persevered in their faith, notwithstanding all the menaces of poverty, of the dungeon, and of utter temporal ruin. Only one year after the revocation, Marshal Vauban wrote,

"France has lost one hundred thousand inhabitants, sixty millions of coined money, nine thousand sailors, twelve thousand disciplined soldiers, six hundred officers, and her most nourishing manufactures."

From this hour the fortunes of Louis XIV. began manifestly to decline. The Protestant population of France at that time was between two and three millions. The edict of revocation was enforced with the utmost severity. Many noble-hearted Catholics sympathized with the Protestants in their dreadful sufferings, and aided them to escape. The tide of emigration flowed steadily from all the provinces. The arrival of the pastors and their flocks upon foreign soil created an indescribable sensation. From all the courts in Protestant Christendom a cry of indignation rose against such cruelty. Though royal guards were posted at the gates of the towns, on the bridges, at the fords of the rivers, and upon all the by-ways which led to the frontiers, and though many thousands were arrested, still many thousands escaped. Some heroic bands fought their way to the frontiers with drawn swords. Some obtained passports from kind-hearted Catholic governors. Some bribed their guards. Some traveled by night, from cavern to cavern, in the garb of merchants, pilgrims, venders of rosaries and chaplets, servants, mendicants.

Thousands perished of cold, hunger, and exhaustion. Thousands were shot by the soldiers. Thousands were seized and condemned to the dungeon or the galleys. The galleys of Marseilles were crowded with these victims of fanatical despotism. Among them were many of the most illustrious men in France, magistrates, nobles, scholars of the highest name and note.

The agitation and emigration were so immense that Louis XIV. became alarmed. Protestant England, Switzerland, Holland, Prussia, Denmark, Sweden, hospitably received the sufferers and contributed generously to the supply of their wants. "Charity," it is said, "draws from an exhaustless fountain. The more it gives the more it has to give."

It is now not possible to estimate the precise number who emigrated. Voltaire says that nearly fifty thousand families left the kingdom, and that they were followed by a great many others. One of the Protestant pastors, Antoine Court, placed the number as high as eight hundred thousand. A Catholic writer, inimical to the Protestants, after carefully consulting the records, states the emigration at two hundred and thirty thousand souls. Of these, 1580 were pastors, 2300 elders, and 15,000 nobles. It is also equally difficult to estimate the numbers who perished in the attempt to escape. M. de Sismondi thinks that as many died as emigrated. He places the number at between three and four hundred thousand.

As we have mentioned, the Protestants were compelled to place their children in Catholic schools, to be taught the Catechism by the priests. A new ordinance was soon issued, which required that the children, between five and sixteen, of all *suspected* of Protestantism, should be taken from their parents and placed in Catholic families. A general search was made throughout the kingdom for all books which could be deemed favorable to the Protestant faith. These were destroyed to the last copy. Thus perished many very valuable works. "The Bible itself, the Bible above all, was confiscated and burned with persevering animosity."[U]

[Footnote U: History of the Protestants of France, by Prof. G. De Félice.]

But there is no power of persecution which can utterly crush out two or three millions of people. There were occasional reactions. Louis XIV. himself became, at times, appalled by the atrocities his dragoons were perpetrating, and he commanded more moderation. In some of the provinces where the Protestants had been greatly in the majority, the king found it very difficult to enforce his despotic and sanguinary code. The persecuted people who could not fly from the kingdom, some having given a compulsory and nominal assent to Catholicism, held secret assemblies in forests, on mountain summits, and in wild ravines. Some of the pastors ventured to return to France, and to assist in these scenes of perilous worship.

"On hearing this, the king, his ministers, and the Jesuits were transported with uncontrollable rage. Sentence of death was pronounced in the month of July, 1686, against the pastors who had returned to France. Those who lent them an asylum, or any assistance whatever, were condemned to the galleys for life. A reward of five thousand five hundred livres was promised to any one who seized or secured the seizure of a minister. The sentence of death was pronounced against all who should be taken in any of these religious assemblies."[V]

[Footnote V: M. G. De Félice.]

Soldiers were sent in all directions to hunt the Protestants. "It was," writes Voltaire, "a chase in a grand cover." If the voice of prayer or of a psalm were heard in any wild retreat, the soldiers opened fire upon the assembly of men, women, and children, and hewed them down without mercy with their blood-stained swords. In several of these encounters, three or four hundred men, women, and young children were left dead and unburied upon the spot.

If any sick persons, apparently near death, refused to receive the sacraments of the Catholic Church from the hands of a Catholic priest, should they recover, they were punished with confiscation of property and consignment to the galleys for life. If they did not recover, their bodies were refused respectful burial, and were dragged on a hurdle and thrown into a ditch, to be devoured by carrion crows.

Many honorable Catholics cried out with horror against these enormities. All humane hearts revolted against such cruelty. The voice of indignant remonstrance rose from every Protestant nation. The French court became embarrassed. Two millions of people could not be put to death. The prisons were filled to suffocation. The galleys were crowded, and could receive no more. Many were transported to America.

The Jansenists remonstrated. The good Catholic bishops of Grenoble and St. Poins boldly addressed the curates of their dioceses, directing them not to force communion upon the Protestants, and forbidding all violence. Many pious curates refused to act the part of accusers, or to torment the dying with their importunities. But the Jesuits and the great mass of the clergy urged on the persecution.

Madame de Maintenon became greatly troubled by these atrocities, against which she did not dare to remonstrate. Louis XIV. was somewhat alarmed by the outcry which these measures aroused from Protestant Europe, but his pride revolted against making the admission, before his subjects and foreign courts, that he could have been guilty of a mistake. He could not endure the thought of humbling himself by a retraction, thus confessing that he had failed in an enterprise upon which he had entered with such determination. Thus influenced, the king, on the 13th of April, 1662, issued a decree solemnly confirming the revocation of the Edict of Nantes. "Not one law of torture and blood was abolished."

The king, meanwhile, urged by his growing passion for Madame de Maintenon, determined to remove from court Madame de Montespan, whom he had come to thoroughly dislike. But he had not the courage to announce his determination in person. He therefore commissioned Madame de Maintenon to make the painful communication. She, shrinking from so unwelcome a task, persuaded the Marquis de Vivonne, brother of the marchioness, to break the tidings to his sister. He invited her to take a ride with him in his carriage, gradually introduced the subject, and at last plainly informed her that she must either, of her own accord, immediately and forever retire from Versailles, or submit to the indignity of being arrested by the police and removed by them.

Madame de Montespan was in a fearful rage. Though fully aware of her waning power over the king, the menace of arrest and banishment was an indignity the thought of which had never entered her mind. But the calm firmness of her brother soon convinced her of the impotence of all exhibitions of indignation. The splendor-loving marchioness was, as we have mentioned already, wealthy. She was, however, informed that the king had decided to settle upon her an annual pension of six hundred thousand livres. When we consider the comparative value of money then and now, it is estimated that this amount was equivalent to about four hundred and eighty thousand dollars at the present day.

"Madame de Montespan," writes Miss Pardoe, "buried her face in her hands, and remained for a considerable time lost in thought. When, at length, she looked up, her lips were pale and her voice trembled. She had not shed a tear, but her breast heaved, and she had evidently come to a decision. Folding her shawl about her, she requested the marquis immediately to drive her to Versailles, it being necessary, as she asserted, that she should collect her money, her jewels, and her papers, after which she declared that she was ready,

KARTINDO PUBLISHING HOUSE (Kartindo.Com)

for the sake of her family, to follow his advice."

[Illustration: PARTERRE OF VERSAILLES.]

They returned to the palace. Madame de Maintenon hastened to her apartments. The Marquis de Vivonne informed her of the success of his mission, and she communicated the intelligence to the king.

The marchioness had been in her apartments but about twenty minutes, when, to her surprise, the door opened, and the king entered unannounced. The marchioness, with her own graphic pen, has given an account of the singular and characteristic interview which ensued.

The king came forward smiling very complacently at the thought that with so little embarrassment he was to get rid of a companion whose presence had become an annoyance to him--that he could discard her as easily as he could lay aside a pair of soiled gloves. He congratulated the marchioness upon the great good sense she had shown in thus readily sundering ties which, after existing for eighteen years, had become embarrassing. He spoke of their children as his property, and assured her that he should do all in his power to promote their welfare; that he had already, by act of Parliament, conferred upon them statute legitimacy, and had thus effaced the dishonor of their birth. He apologized for not having her name mentioned in Parliament as their mother, this being impracticable, since she was the wife of another man.

With smiling complacency, as if he were communicating very gratifying intelligence, he informed this crushed and discarded mother that, since her children were now princes, they would, of course, reside at court, and that she, their dishonored mother, might occasionally be permitted to visit them--that he would issue an order to that effect. And, finally, he coolly advised her to write to her husband, whom she had abandoned eighteen years ago, soliciting a renewal of their relationship, with the assurance that it was her intention to return to the paths of virtue.

Almost gasping with indignation, the haughty marchioness succeeded in restraining herself until the king had finished his harangue. She then burst forth in a reply which astonished and even alarmed the king.

"I am amazed," said she, "at the indifference with which a monarch, who boasts of his magnanimity, can throw from him a woman who has sacrificed every thing to his pleasure. For two years your majesty, in devotion to others, has been estranged from me, and yet never have I publicly offered one word of expostulation. Why is it, then, that I am now, after silently submitting for two years to this estrangement, to be ignominiously banished from the court? Still, my position here has become so hateful, through the perfidy and treachery of those by whom I am compelled to associate, that I will willingly consent never again to approach the person of the king upon condition that the odious woman who has supplanted me[W] shall also be exiled."

[Footnote W: Madame de Maintenon.]

The proud monarch was enraged. Pale with anger, he replied, "The kings of Europe have never yet ventured to dictate laws in my palace, nor shall you, madame, subject me to yours. The lady whom I have too long suffered you to offend is as nobly born as yourself. If you were instrumental in opening the gates of the palace to her, you thus introduced there gentleness, talent, and virtue. This lady, whom you have upon every occasion slandered, has lost no opportunity to excuse and justify you. She will remain near the court which her fathers defended, and which her wise councils now strengthen. In seeking to remove you from the court, where your presence and pretensions have long since been misplaced, I wished to spare you the evidence of an *event* calculated to irritate your already exasperated nature. But stay you here, madame," he added, sarcastically, "stay you here, since you love great catastrophes and are amused by them. Day after to-morrow you will be more than ever a *supernumerary* in the palace."

This heartless announcement, that Madame de Maintenon was to take the place of Madame de Montespan in the affections of the king, and probably as his wedded wife, pierced, as with a dagger's point, the heart of the discarded favorite. She fell senseless to the floor. The king, without the slightest exhibition of sympathy, looked on impatiently, while her women, who were immediately summoned, endeavored to restore consciousness. As the unhappy marchioness revived, the first words which fell upon her ears were from the king, as he said,

"All this wearies me beyond endurance. She must leave the palace this very day."

In a frenzy of rage and despair, the marchioness seized a dessert-knife which chanced to lay upon the table, and, springing from the arms of her attendants, rushed upon her youngest child, the little Count de Toulouse, whom the king held by the hand, and from whom she was to be cruelly severed, and endeavored to plunge the knife into his bosom, exclaiming,

"Yes, I will leave this palace, but first--"

At that moment, before the sentence was finished, the door opened, and Madame de Maintenon, who had probably anticipated some tragic scene, sprang upon the wretched woman, seizing the knife with one hand, and with the other thrusting the child away. The maniacal marchioness was seized by her attendants. The king tottered to the chimney-piece, buried his face in his hands, and, from a complicity of emotions not easily disentangled, wept convulsively.

Madame de Maintenon's hand was cut by the knife. As she was binding up the bleeding wound with her handkerchief, the half-delirious marchioness said to her, referring to the fact that the king had at first been unwilling to receive her as the guardian of the children,

"Ah! madame, had I believed what the king told me fourteen years ago, my life would not have been in your power to-day."

Madame de Maintenon, her eyes suffused with tears, looked sadly upon her, then taking her hand, pressed it feelingly, and, without uttering a word, left the apartment. The king followed her. The heart-broken marchioness, in most imploring tones, entreated the king not thus to leave her. He paid no heed to her supplications. The agitation of this scene threw Madame de Montespan into such a burning fever that for several days she could not be removed from her bed of pain and woe.

CHAPTER X

THE SECRET MARRIAGE

1685-1689

Temptation resisted.--Rumors of marriage.--Preparations for the marriage.--The archbishop summoned.--An extraordinary scene.--Ceremonies.--The *Widow Scarron*.--Etiquette.--Humiliation of Madame de Montespan.--Routine of a day at Versailles.--The *First Entrée*.--The ceremony of dressing.--The *Grand Entrée*.--Dressing the king.--The royal breakfast.--Formalities.--The dressing completed.--The king prays.--The king attends mass.--Etiquette at the royal dinner.--Visits the kennel.--The morning drive.--The royal supper.--Tasting and trying.--"Drink for the king!"--He feeds his dogs at midnight.--Madame de Maintenon's apartments.--Her tact.--Sickness of the king.--A surgical operation necessary.--World-weariness of the king.--Dissatisfied with Versailles.--The royal palaces unsatisfactory.--The "hermitage" at Marly.--War with Germany.--The dauphin in command.--Devastation of the Palatinate.--Designs upon England.--Civil war in France.--Complications of the royal family.

The king exerted all his powers of persuasion to induce Madame de Maintenon to enter into the same relations with him which Madame de Montespan had occupied. At last she declared, in reply to some passionate reproaches on his part, that she should be under the necessity of withdrawing from the court and retiring to the cloister, rather than continue to expose herself to a temptation which was destroying her peace of mind and undermining her health. Under these circumstances the king had been led to think of a private marriage. At first his pride revolted from the thought. But in no other way could he secure Madame de Maintenon.

Rumors of the approaching marriage were circulated through the court. The dauphin expostulated with his father most earnestly against it, and succeeded in inducing the king to consult the Abbé Fenelon and Louvois. They both protested against the measure as compromising the dignity of the monarch and the interests of the nation. Bossuet, however, urged the marriage. Boldly he warned the king against entering again into such connections as those which had hitherto sullied his life, wounded his reputation, and endangered his eternal welfare.

KARTINDO PUBLISHING HOUSE (Kartindo.Com)

Pure as Madame de Maintenon was, the devotion of the king to her was so marked that her reputation began to suffer. She felt the unjust imputations cast upon her very keenly. The king at last resolved that it should be so no longer. Having come to a decision, he acted very promptly. It was a cold night in January, 1686. A smothering snow-storm swept the streets of Paris. At half past ten o'clock a court messenger entered the archiepiscopal palace with a sealed packet, requesting the archbishop to repair immediately to Versailles to perform the marriage ceremony. The great clock of the Cathedral was tolling the hour of eleven as the prelate entered his carriage in the darkness and the storm. At half past twelve he reached the gate of the chateau. Here Bontems, the first valet de chambre of the king, conducted the archbishop to the private closet of his majesty. Madame de Maintenon was there in full dress. Louis XIV. stood by her side. In the same apartment were the Marquis de Montechevreuil and the king's confessor, Père la Chaise.

Miss Pardoe thus describes the scene that ensued:

"As the eye of the king rested upon the archbishop, he exclaimed, 'Let us go.' Taking the hand of the lady, he led her forward through the long suite of rooms, followed by the other actors in this extraordinary scene, who moved on in profound silence, thrown for an instant into broad light by the torch carried by Bontems, and then suddenly lost in the deep darkness beyond its influence. Nothing was to be heard as the bridal party proceeded save the muffled sound of their footsteps, deadened by the costly carpets over which they trod. But it was remarked that as the light flashed for an instant across the portraits of his family which clothed the walls, Louis XIV. glanced eagerly and somewhat nervously upon them, as though he dreaded the rebuke of some stern eye or haughty lip for the weakness of which he was about to become guilty."

The marriage ceremony was performed by the Archbishop of Paris. There were eight persons present as witnesses, most of them of high distinction. The king was in the forty-eighth year of his age, and Madame de Maintenon in her fifty-second. The marriage was celebrated with all the established ceremonies of the Church, the solemnization of the mass, the exchange of marriage rings, and the pronouncing of the benediction by the archbishop. A magnificent suite of apartments was prepared for Madame de Maintenon at Versailles. She retained her own liveries, but thenceforward appeared in public only in the carriage of the king. Though by her own private attendants she was addressed as "your majesty," she was never publicly recognized as the queen. The king addressed her simply as *Madame.*

Though the morning after the nuptials the astounding rumor spread through the court that the king had actually married the *Widow Scarron*, still there were no positive vouchers found for the fact. As she was never recognized as the queen, for a long time many doubts rested upon the reality of the marriage.

It was a matter of necessity that Madame de Montespan should call upon Madame de Maintenon, and pay her respects to her as the real though unrecognized wife of the monarch. Dressed in her richest robes, and glittering with jewels, the discarded favorite entered the apartment of her hated rival. The king was seated by her side. His majesty rose, bowed formally, and took his seat. Madame de Maintenon did not rise, but, with a slight flush upon her cheek, motioned to Madame de Montespan to take a seat upon a *tabouret* which stood near by. The king scarcely noticed her. Madame de Maintenon addressed her in a few words of condescension. The unhappy visitor, after a short struggle to regain her composure, rose from the humble stool upon which she had been seated, and, repeating the stately reverences which etiquette required, withdrew from the room.

With crushed heart she retired to her apartment, and, weeping bitterly, threw herself upon a sofa. She soon sent for her son, the Duke du Maine, hoping to hear, from his lips at least, words of sympathy. But the duke, who had reproached his mother with his dishonorable birth, and who, by a royal decree, had been recognized as a prince, was not at all disposed to cultivate intimate relations with that mother, now that the memory of disgrace only would be perpetuated by that recognition. Without the exhibition of the slightest emotion, the duke addressed his mother in a few cold, formal words, and left her. The marchioness summoned her carriage, and left Versailles and the court forever. As she cast a last look upon the palace, she saw the king standing at the balcony of a window watching her departure.

The reader will be interested in learning the routine of a day as passed by this most sumptuous of earthly kings amidst the splendors of Versailles. At eight o'clock in the morning the under valets carefully entered the bedchamber, opened the shutters, replenished the wood fire, if cold, and removed the ample refreshments which were always placed by the royal bedside in case the king should need food during the night.

The first valet then entered, carefully dressed, and took his stand respectfully by the side of the bed-curtains. At half past eight precisely he drew the curtains and awoke the king, assuming always that he was asleep. The valet then immediately retired to an adjoining room, where several distinguished members

KARTINDO PUBLISHING HOUSE (Kartindo.Com)

of the court were in waiting, and communicated to them the important intelligence that the king no longer slept.

The folding doors were thrown open, and the dauphin, attended by his two sons, the eldest of whom was entitled *Monsieur*, and the youngest the Duke of Chartres, entered, and inquired of the king how he had passed the night. They were immediately followed by the Duke du Maine and the Count de Toulouse, sons of Madame de Montespan, and by the first lord of the bedchamber and the grand master of the robes. They were succeeded by the first valet of the wardrobe, and by several officers, each bearing a portion of the royal vestments. The two medical attendants of the king, the physician and surgeon, also entered at the same time.

The king, still remaining pillowed in his gorgeous bed, held out his hands, and his first valet de chambre poured upon them a few drops of spirits of wine, holding beneath them a basin of silver. The first lord of the bedchamber presented a vase of holy water, with which the king made the sign of the cross upon his brow and breast. His majesty then repeated a short prayer. A collection of wigs was presented to him. He selected the one which he wished to wear. As the king rose from his couch, the first lord of the bedchamber drew upon him his dressing-gown, which was always a richly embroidered and costly robe.

The king then sat down, and, holding out one sacred foot after the other, his valet, Bontems, drew on his stockings and his slippers of embroidered velvet. The monarch condescended to place upon his head, with his own hand, the wig which he had selected. Again the devout monarch crossed himself with holy water, and, emerging from the balustrade which inclosed the bed, seated himself in a large arm-chair. He was now prepared for what was called *The First Entrée*.

The chief lord of the bedchamber, with a loud voice, announced *The First Entrée*. A number of courtiers, who were peculiarly favored, were then admitted to the distinguished honor of seeing his majesty washed and shaved. The barber of the king removed his beard and gently washed his face with a sponge saturated with spirits of wine and water. The king himself wiped his face with a soft towel, while Bontems held the glass before him.

And now the master of the robes approached to dress the king. Those who had been present at what was called the *petit lever* retired. A new set of dignitaries, of higher name and note, crowded the anteroom to enjoy the signal honor of being present at the *Grand Entrée*, that is, of witnessing the sublime ceremony of seeing shirt, trowsers, and frock placed upon his sacred majesty.

Three of the highest officers of the court stood at the door, attended by several valets and door-keepers of the cabinet. Admission to the *Grand Entrée* was considered so great an honor that even princes sought it, and often in vain.

As each individual presented himself, his name was whispered to the first lord of the bedchamber, who repeated it to the king. When the monarch made no reply the visitor was admitted, and the duke walked back to his station near the fireplace, where he marshaled the new-comers to their several places in order to prevent their pressing too closely about his majesty. Princes and governors, marshals and peers, were alike subjected to this tedious and somewhat humiliating ceremony, from which three individuals alone were excepted, Racine, Boileau, and Mansard. On their arrival at the guarded door they simply scratched against the panel, when the usher threw open the folding door, and they stood in the presence of the monarch.

[Illustration: RACINE AND BOILEAU.]

In the mean time, a valet of the wardrobe delivered to a gentleman of the chamber the socks and garters, which the *gentleman* presented to the monarch, and which socks his majesty deigned to draw on himself. Even with his own hand he clasped the garters with their diamond buckles. Etiquette did not allow the king to unclasp them at night. The head valet de chambre enjoyed the privilege of unclasping the garter of the right leg, while a more humble attendant performed the same office for the left leg.

A distinguished officer of the household presented the monarch with his *haut de chausses* (breeches), to which silk stockings were attached; the king drew them on; another gentleman put on his shoes; another gentleman buckled them. Two pages, richly dressed in crimson velvet embroidered with gold, removed the slippers which the king had laid aside.

And now came the royal breakfast. Two officers of the household entered, in picturesque attire, one bearing a loaf of bread on an enameled salver, and another a folded napkin between two enameled plates. The royal cup-bearer handed a golden vase, richly decorated, to one of the lords. He poured into it a small quantity of wine and water. Another lord tasted of it, to prove that it

KARTINDO PUBLISHING HOUSE (Kartindo.Com)

contained no poison. The vase was then carefully rinsed, and being again filled with the wine and water, was presented to the king on a gold salver.

His majesty drank. Then the dauphin, who was always present at these solemnities, handed his hat and gloves to the first lord in waiting, and presented the monarch with a napkin with which to wipe his lips. Breakfast was a very frugal repast. Having partaken of these slight refreshments, the king laid aside his dressing-gown. One of his lordly attendants then assisted him in removing his night-shirt by the left sleeve. It was Bontems's peculiar privilege to draw it off by the right sleeve.

The royal shirt, which had been carefully warmed, was then given to the first lord. He presented it to the dauphin, who approached and presented it to the king. Some one of the higher lords, previously designated for the honor, assisted the king in the arrangement of his shirt and breeches. A duke enjoyed the honor of putting on his inner waistcoat. Two valets presented the king with his sword, vest, and blue ribbon. A nobleman then stepped forward and buckled on the sword, assisted in putting on the vest, and placed over his shoulders a scarf bearing the cross of the Holy Ghost in diamonds, and the cross of St. Louis.

The king then drew on his under coat, with the assistance of the grand master of the robes, adjusted his cravat of rich lace, which was folded round his neck by a favorite courtier, and finally emptied into the pockets of the loose outer coat, which was presented to him for that purpose, the contents of those which he had worn the previous day. He then received two handkerchiefs of costly point from another attendant, by whom they were carried on an enameled saucer of oval shape called salve. His toilet once completed, Louis XIV. returned to the *ruelle* of his bed, where he knelt down upon two cushions already prepared for him, and said his prayers; all the bishops and cardinals entering within the balustrade in his suite, and reciting their devotional exercises in a suppressed voice.

The king, being thus dressed, retired from his chamber to his cabinet. He was followed, in solemn procession, by all those dignitaries of Church and State who had enjoyed the privilege of the *Grand Entrée*. He then issued the orders of the day, after which all withdrew excepting some of his children, whom a royal decree had legitimatized and raised to the rank of princes, with their former tutors or governors.

In the mean time a crowd of courtiers were assembled in the great gallery of Versailles, to accompany the king to mass. The captain of the royal guard awaited orders at the door of the cabinet. At 12 o'clock the door was thrown open, and the king, followed by a splendid retinue, proceeded to the chapel.

The service was short. At one o'clock the king returned to his room, and dined sumptuously and alone. He was waited upon, at the table, by the first gentleman of the chamber. Sometimes the dauphin or other lords of highest rank were present, but they stood respectfully at a distance. No one was permitted to be seated in the royal presence. The brother of the king stood at times by the chair of his majesty, holding his napkin for him. Upon the king's twice requesting him to be seated, he was permitted to take a seat upon a stool, behind the king, still holding his napkin.

Upon rising from the table the king repaired to the grand saloon, where he tarried for a few moments, that persons of high distinction, who enjoyed the privilege of addressing him, might have an opportunity to do so. He then returned to his cabinet. The door was closed, and the king had a brief interview with his children, of whom he was very fond. He then repaired to the kennel of his dogs, of whom he was also fond, and amused himself, for a time, in feeding them and playing with them.

He now made some slight change in his dress. A small number of persons, of high rank, enjoyed the distinguished honor of being present in his chamber as the monarch, with all suitable stateliness of ceremony, exchanged one royal garment for another. The carriage awaited the king in the marble court. He descended by a private staircase. His craving for fresh air was such that he took a drive whatever the weather. Scarcely any degree of heat or cold, or floods of rain, could prevent him from his drive, or his stag-hunt, or his overlooking the workmen. Sometimes the ladies of his court rode out with him on picnic excursions to the forests of Fontainebleau or Marly.

Upon returning from the drive, the king again changed his dress and repaired to his cabinet. He then proceeded to the apartments of Madame de Maintenon, where he remained conversing with her, or reading, and sometimes transacting business with his minister, until ten o'clock. The hour for supper had now arrived. The house-steward, with his badge of office in hand, gave the information to the captain of the guard. He, entering the royal presence from the antechamber, announced the fact to the king, and opened wide the door. After the delay of a quarter of an hour, which etiquette required, his majesty advanced to the supper-room. During the quarter of an hour which had elapsed,

KARTINDO PUBLISHING HOUSE (Kartindo.Com)

the officers of the household had made preparations for the royal repast by tasting the bread and the salt, and by testing the plates, the fork, the spoon, the knife, and the tooth-pick of the king, so as to be assured that no poison could be thus conveyed.

As the king, preceded by the house-steward and two ushers with flambeaux, entered the supper-room, he found there awaiting him the princes and princesses of France, with a numerous assemblage of courtiers, gentlemen, and ladies. The king, having taken his seat, requested the others to be seated also. Six noblemen immediately stationed themselves at each end of the table, to wait upon the king. Each one, as he presented a dish to the king, first tasted of it himself. When the king wished for a drink, his cup-bearer exclaimed aloud, "Drink for the king." Two of the principal officers, making a profound obeisance, approached his majesty, one bearing an enameled cup and two decanters upon a salver. The other poured out the wine, tasted it, and presented the goblet to the king. With another low salutation, the two officers replaced the decanters upon the sideboard.

The repast being finished, the king rose, and, preceded by two guards and an usher, and followed by all the company, proceeded to the bedchamber. He there bowed adieu to the company, and, entering the cabinet, took a seat in a large arm-chair. The members of the royal family were introduced. His brother, Monsieur, was permitted to take an arm-chair. All the rest remained standing except the princesses, who were indulged with stools. After an hour or so of such converse as these stately forms would admit, the king, about midnight, went again to feed his dogs. He then retired to his chamber, with great pomp said his prayers, and was undressed and put to bed with ceremonies similar to those with which he had been dressed in the morning.

Such was the ordinary routine of the life of the king at Versailles. Its dreary monotony was broken by occasional fêtes, balls, and theatric shows. Madame de Maintenon testifies to the almost insupportable tedium of such a life. "If you could only," she exclaims, "form an idea of what it is!"

Magnificent apartments were prepared for Madame de Maintenon at Versailles, opposite the suite of rooms occupied by the king. Similar arrangements were made for her in all the royal palaces. Royalty alone could occupy arm-chairs in the presence of the sovereign. In each of her apartments there were two such, one for the king and the other for herself. The king often transacted business with his minister, Louvois, in her room. She had sufficient tact never to express an opinion, or to take a part in the conversation except when appealed to.

Madame de Maintenon was exceedingly anxious that the king should publicly recognize her as his wife. It is said that the king, tormented by the embarrassments which the secret marriage had brought upon him, seriously contemplated this. His minister, Louvois, remonstrated even passionately against such a recognition. At the close of a painful interview upon this subject, he threw himself upon his knees before his majesty, and, presenting to him the hilt of a small sword which the minister usually wore, exclaimed,

"Take my life, sire, that I may not become the witness of a disgrace which will dishonor your majesty in the eyes of all Europe."

Others of the most influential members of the court joined in the opposition, and so strenuously that the king commanded Madame de Maintenon never again to allude to the subject.

Premature old age was fast advancing upon the king, though he had as yet attained only his forty-ninth year. He was tortured by the gout. He was also attacked by a very painful and dangerous internal malady. His sufferings were dreadful. It became necessary for him to submit to a perilous surgical operation. The king met the crisis with much heroism. Four persons only, including Madame de Maintenon, were present during the operation. Indeed, the greatest precautions had been adopted to keep the fact that an operation was to be performed a profound secret. During the operation the king uttered not a groan. It was successful. In gratitude he conferred upon the skillful operator who had relieved him from anguish and saved his life an estate valued at more than fifty thousand crowns.

Weary of every thing else, the king now sought to find some little interest in building. The renowned architect, Mansard, whose genius still embellishes our most beautiful edifices, was commissioned to erect a pavilion on the grounds of Versailles in imitation of an Italian villa. Thus rose, within a year, the *Grand Trianon*, which subsequently became so celebrated as the favorite rural residence of Maria Antoinette.

[Illustration: THE TRIANON.]

[Illustration: MARLY.]

Most men who, with vast wealth, attempt to build a mansion which shall eclipse that of all their neighbors, and which shall be perfect in all the appliances of comfort and luxury, find themselves, in the end, bitterly disappointed. This was pre-eminently the case with Louis XIV. The palace of Versailles, still unfinished, had already cost him countless millions. But it did not please the king. It had cold and cheerless grandeur, but no attractions as a home. The king looked with weary eyes upon the mountain pile of marble which had risen at his bidding, and found it about as uncongenial for a home as would be the Cathedral of Notre Dame. Disgusted with the etiquette which enslaved him, satiated with sensual indulgence, and having exhausted all the fountains of worldly pleasure, with waning powers of body and of mind, it is not possible that any thing could have satisfied the world-weary king.

He had other palaces. None suited him. The Tuileries and the Louvre were in the heart of the noisy city. The banqueting hall at St. Germain overlooked the sepulchre of St. Denis, where the grave-worm held its banquet. Fontainebleau was at too great a distance from the capital. To reach it required a carriage drive of four or five hours. Vincennes, notwithstanding the grandeur of the antique, time-worn castle, was gloomy in its surroundings, inconvenient in its internal arrangements--a prison rather than a palace.

About nine miles from Paris, upon the left bank of the Seine, there reposed the silent village of Marly. The king selected that as the spot upon which he would rear a snug "hermitage" to which he could retire "from noise and tumult far." The passion for building is a fearful passion, which often involves its victim in ruin. The plans of the king expanded under his eye. The little hermitage became a spacious palace, where a court could be entertained with all the appliances of regal elegance.

But dark and stormy days were rapidly gathering around the path of the king. He became involved in war with Germany. The complicated reasons can scarcely be unraveled. The king sent his son, the dauphin, at the head of one hundred thousand men, to invade Holland. Situated upon both sides of the Rhine there was a territory called the Palatinate. It embraced one thousand five hundred and ninety square miles, being not quite so large as the State of Delaware. It contained an intelligent, industrious, and prosperous population of a little over three hundred thousand. The beautiful city of Manheim was the capital of the province.

Though the dauphin was nominally at the head of the invading army, that the glory of its victories might redound to his name, the ablest of the French generals were associated with him, and they, in reality, took the direction of affairs. One city after another speedily fell into the hands of the French. The king mercilessly resolved, and without any justification whatever, to convert the whole province into a desert. An order was issued by the king that every city, village, castle, and hut should be laid in ashes.

It was midwinter--the month of February, 1689. There were many beautiful cities in the province, such as Manheim, Philipsbourg, Franckendal, Spire, Treves, Worms, and Oppendeim. There were more than fifty feudal castles in the territory, the ancestral homes of noble families. The citizens had but short warning. Houses, furniture, food, all were consumed. The flames rose to heaven, calling upon God for vengeance. Smouldering ruins every where met the eye. Men, women, and children wandered starving through the fields.

Nearly all Europe soon became banded against this haughty monarch, and he found it necessary to raise an army of four hundred thousand men to meet the exigencies.

Intoxicated by the pride of past success, he thought that he should be able to force upon England a Roman Catholic king, and the Roman Catholic faith, and thus expel *heresy* from England, as he dreamed that he had expelled it from France. He equipped a fleet, and manned it with twenty thousand soldiers, to force upon the British people King James II., whom they had indignantly discarded.

Civil war was now also desolating unhappy France. The Protestants, bereft of their children, robbed of their property, driven from their homes, dragged to the galleys, plunged into dungeons, broken upon the wheel, hanged upon scaffolds, rose in several places in the most desperate insurrectionary bands. And the man who was thus crushing beneath the heel of his armies the quivering hearts of the Palatinate, and who was drenching his own realms with tears and blood, was clothed in purple, and faring sumptuously, and reclining upon the silken sofas of Marly and Versailles. It is not strange that Faith, with uplifted hands and gushing eyes, should have exclaimed, "O Lord, how long!"

The singular complication of the royal family, with the various mothers and the various children, some of which children were recognized by royal decree as princes, and some of whom were not, filled the palaces with bickerings, envyings, and discontent in every form. The unhappy dauphiness, who had long been immersed in the profoundest gloom, at last found a welcome retreat in the grave. Neither her husband nor the king shed a single tear over her remains, which were hurried to the vaults of St. Denis.

KARTINDO PUBLISHING HOUSE (Kartindo.Com)

CHAPTER XI

INTRIGUES AND WARS

1690-1711

Exhaustion of the treasury.--The royal plate sacrificed.--Assumptions of Louvois.--Disgrace, sickness, and death of Louvois.--Louis suspicious of Madame de Maintenon.--Letters.--Court life.--The dauphin.--His sons.--Graces of the Duchess of Burgoyne.--Misery of the people.--Extravagance of the court.--Brilliant assembly.--Death of Charles II.--The Duke of Anjou proclaimed King of Spain.--Anecdote of the princes.--Preparations for the coronation.--Exultation of Louis XIV.--Final meeting of the royal family.--Last interview between Madame de Montespan and the king.--Penance of Madame de Montespan.--Her death.--Heartless conduct of the king.--His health failing.-- Quarrel with Philip.--He is stricken with apoplexy.--Death of the king's brother.--The king dispels his gloom.--The Princess des Ursins.--Civil war.-- Insurrection of the Protestants.--Enthusiasm of the Camisards.--Cruelty of the persecutors.--Distress in France.--The dauphin taken sick.--Death and burial of the dauphin.

The treasury of the king was empty. Extravagant building, a voluptuous court, and all the enormous expenses of civil and foreign wars, had quite exhausted the finances of the realm. It became necessary to call upon the cities for contributions. New offices were invented, which were imposed upon the wealthy citizens, and for which they were compelled to pay large sums. Even the massive silver plate and furniture, which had attracted the admiration of all visitors to Versailles, were sent to the Mint and coined. Most of the value of these articles of ornament consisted of the skill with which the materials had been wrought into forms of beauty. In melting them down, all this was sacrificed, and nothing remained but the mere value of the metal. Large as were the sums attained by these means, they were but trifling compared with the necessities of the state.

Louvois, the minister of Louis, had for a long time held the reins of government. It was through his influence that the king had been instigated to revoke the Edict of Nantes, to order the dragonnades, and to authorize those atrocities of persecution which must ever expose the name of Louis XIV. to the

KARTINDO PUBLISHING HOUSE (Kartindo.Com)

execrations of humanity. It was Louvois who, from merely contemptible caprice, plunged France into war with Germany. It was through his persuasions that the king was induced to order the utter devastation of the Palatinate.

But the influence of Louvois was now on the wane. The jealous king became weary of his increasingly haughty assumptions. The conflagration of the Palatinate raised a cry of indignation which the king could not but hear. The city of Treves had escaped the flames. Louvois solicited an order to burn it. The king refused to give his consent. Louvois insolently gave the order himself. He then informed the king that he had done so that he might spare the conscience of the king the pain of issuing such an edict.

[Illustration: LOUIS XIV. DIRECTING THE SIEGE.]

Louis was furious. In his rage he forgot all the restraints of etiquette. He seized from the fireplace the tongs, and would have broken the head of the minister had not Madame de Maintenon rushed between them. The king ordered a messenger immediately to be dispatched to countermand the order. He declared that if a single house were burned, the head of the minister should be the forfeit. The city was saved.

In 1691 the French army was besieging Mons. The king visited the works. The haughty minister, unintimidated even by the menace of the tongs, ventured to countermand an order which the king had issued. The lowering brow of the monarch convinced him that his ministerial reign was soon to close.

The health of the minister began rapidly to fail. He became emaciate, languid, and deeply depressed. A few subsequent interviews with the king satisfied him that his disgrace and ruin were decided upon. Indeed, the king had already drawn up the *lettre de cachet* which was to consign him to the Bastile. About the middle of June, 1691, Louvois met the king in his council chamber, and, though the monarch was unusually complaisant, Louvois so thoroughly understood him that he retired to his residence in utter despair. Scarcely had he entered his apartment ere he dropped dead upon the floor. Whether his death were caused by apoplexy, or by poison administered by his own hand or that of others, can never be known. The king forbade all investigation of the case.

Immediately after the death of Louvois, the king began to devote himself to business with an energy which he had never before manifested. Madame de Maintenon made some farther efforts to induce him to proclaim their marriage, but she soon perceived that nothing would induce him to change his resolution, and she accepted the situation. Louis now yielded more than ever to her influence; but he was always apprehensive that she might be engaged in some secret intrigue, and kept a vigilant watch over her. In letters to a friend, she gives some account of her splendid misery.

"The king is perpetually on guard over me. I see no one. He never leaves my room. I am compelled to rise at five in the morning in order to write to you. I experience more than ever that there is no compensation for the loss of liberty."

Again she writes, in reference to the weary routine of court life: "The princesses who have not attended the hunt will come in, followed by their cabal, and wait the return of the king in my apartment in order to go to dinner. The hunters will come in a crowd, and will relate the whole history of their day's sport, without sparing us a single detail. They will then go to dinner. Madame de Dangeau will challenge me, with a yawn, to a game of backgammon. Such is the way in which people live at court."

It will be remembered that the king and queen had an only son, the dauphin. He was a man of ignoble character and of feeble mind. Still, as heir to the throne, he was, next to the king, the most important personage in the realm. The dauphin had three sons, who were in the direct line of succession to the crown. These were Louis, duke of Burgoyne, Philip, duke of Anjou, and Charles, duke of Berri.

The eldest, the Duke of Burgoyne, who, of course, next to the dauphin, was heir to the throne, was thirteen years of age. The king selected for his wife Adelaide, the daughter of the Duke of Savoy, a remarkably graceful, beautiful, and intelligent child of eleven years. The pretty little girl was brought to France to spend a few months in the court previous to her marriage, which was to take place as soon as she should attain her twelfth year. She came in great splendor, with her retinue, her court, and her ladies of honor. Both the king and Madame de Maintenon were charmed with the princess. Sumptuous apartments were assigned her in the palace of Versailles. Madame de Maintenon wrote to the Duchess of Savoy,

"The king is enchanted with her. He expatiates on her deportment, her grace, her courtesy, her reserve, and her modesty. She has all the graces of girlhood, with the perfections of a more mature age. Her temper appears as perfect as her figure promises one day to become. She only requires to speak to display the extent of her intellect. I can not resist thanking your royal highness for giving us a child who, according to all appearance, will be the delight of the court, and the glory of the century."

The king resolved that the festivities at the marriage of these two children should be the most splendid which France had ever witnessed. He announced the intention of appearing himself, upon the occasion, in the most sumptuous apparel which the taste and art of the times could furnish. This intimation was sufficient for the courtiers. Preparations were made for such a display of folly and extravagance as even alarmed the king. All ordinary richness of dress, of satin, and velvet, and embroidery of gold, was discarded for fabrics of unprecedented costliness, for bouquets of diamonds, and wreaths of the most precious gems.

"I can not understand," exclaimed the king, "how husbands are mad enough to suffer themselves to be ruined by the folly of their wives."

The marriage took place between the bride of twelve years and the bridegroom of fourteen at six o'clock in the evening of the 7th of December, 1697. The ceremony was performed in the chapel of the palace at Versailles. The ensuing festivals exceeded in magnificence all that Versailles had previously witnessed. But there was no rejoicing among the people. They listened, some silently, some sullenly, some murmuringly, to the chiming bells and the booming cannon. The elements of discontent and wrath were slowly beginning to collect for bursting forth one hundred years later, in that most sublime of moral tempests, the French Revolution.

The grand avenue to Versailles day after day was crowded with gorgeous equipages. At night it blazed with illuminations. The highest ingenuity was taxed to devise new scenes of splendor and amusement, which followed each other in rapid succession. Three days after the marriage, the king gave a special assembly which was to eclipse all the rest. All the ladies were directed to appear in dresses of black velvet, that the precious gems, which were almost literally to cover those dresses, might sparkle more brilliantly. The great gallery of Versailles was illuminated by four thousand wax-lights. The young bride wore upon her apron alone jewels estimated at a sum equal to fifty thousand dollars.

On the 1st of November, 1700, Charles II., the half crazed King of Spain, died, leaving no heir. The pope, Innocent XII., bribed by Louis XIV., sent a nuncio

KARTINDO PUBLISHING HOUSE (Kartindo.Com)

to the dying king, enjoining upon him to transmit his crown to the children of the Dauphin of France, as the legitimate heirs to the monarchy. As the Duke of Burgoyne was the direct heir to the throne of France, the second son of the dauphin, the Duke of Anjou, still a mere boy, was proclaimed King of Spain, with the title of Philip V.

On the 14th of the month the Spanish embassador was summoned to an audience with Louis XIV. at Versailles. The king presented his grandson to the minister, saying, "This, sir, is the Duke of Anjou, whom you may salute as your king."

A large crowd of courtiers was soon assembled. The Spanish minister threw himself upon his knees before the boy with expressions of profound homage. There was a scene of great excitement. The king, embracing with his left arm the neck of the young prince, pointed to him with his right hand, and said to those present,

"Gentlemen, this is the King of Spain. His birth calls him to the crown.[X] The late king has recognized his right by his will. All the nation desires his succession, and has entreated it at my hands. It is the will of Heaven, to which I conform with satisfaction."

[Footnote X: The claim of the young prince was founded upon the fact that his grandmother, Maria Theresa, was the eldest daughter of Philip IV. of Spain. She had, however, upon her marriage, renounced all claim to the succession. Her younger sister, Margarita, had married the Emperor Leopold of Austria without this renunciation. The emperor claimed the crown for her daughter, who had married the Elector of Bavaria. Hence the war of *The Spanish Succession.*]

The Duke of Anjou was quite delighted in finding himself thus liberated from all the restraints of tutors and governors, and of being, in his boyhood, elevated to the dignity of a crowned king. As soon as these stately forms of etiquette were concluded, and he was alone with his brothers, he kicked up his heels and snapped his fingers, exclaiming with delight,

"So I am King of Spain. You, Burgoyne, will be King of France. And you, my poor Berri, are the only one who must live and die a subject."

The little prince replied, perhaps upon the principle that "the grapes were sour," perhaps because he had observed how little real happiness regal state had brought to his grandfather,

"That fact will not grieve me. I shall have less trouble and more pleasure than either of you. I shall enjoy the right of hunting both in France and Spain, and can follow a wolf from Paris to Madrid."

Preparations were immediately made for the departure of the boy-king to take possession of his Spanish throne and crown. The pomp-loving French king had decided to invest the occasion with great splendor. He regarded it as a signal stroke of policy, and a great victory on his part, that he had been enabled, notwithstanding the remonstrances of other nations, to place a French Bourbon prince upon the throne of Spain, thus virtually uniting the two nations. He thought he had thus extended the domain of France to the Straits of Gibraltar. "Henceforth," exclaimed Louis XIV., exultingly, "there are no more Pyrenees."

To his grandson, the new king, he said, "Be a good Spaniard, but never forget that you were born a Frenchman. Carefully maintain the union of the two nations. Thus only can you render them both happy."

There was a final meeting of the royal family to take leave of the young monarch as he was departing for his realm. All the young nobility of France, with a numerous military escort, were to compose his brilliant retinue. The Duchess du Maine, the legitimatized daughter of Madame de Montespan, and thus the half brother of the dauphin, persuaded the dauphin to invite her mother to the palace on this occasion. Here occurred the last interview between the heartless king and his discarded favorite.

As the king made the tour of the room, he found himself opposite Madame de Montespan. She was greatly overcome by her emotions, and, pale and trembling, was near fainting. The king coldly and searchingly, for a moment, fixed his eye upon her, and then said, calmly,

"Madame, I congratulate you. You are still as handsome and attractive as ever. I hope that you are also happy."

The marchioness replied, "At this moment, sire, I am very happy, since I have the honor of presenting my respectful homage to your majesty."

KARTINDO PUBLISHING HOUSE (Kartindo.Com)

The king, with his studied grace of courtesy, kissed her hand, and continued his progress around the circle. The monarch and his perhaps equally guilty victim never met again. She lived twenty-two years after her expulsion from the palace. They were twenty-two years of joylessness. Her confessor, who seems to have been a man of sincere piety, refused her absolution until she had written to her husband, the Marquis de Montespan, whom she had abandoned for the guilty love of the king, affirming her heartfelt repentance, imploring his forgiveness, and entreating him either to receive her back, or to order her to any place of residence which he should think proper. The indignant marquis replied that he would neither admit her to his house, nor prescribe for her any future rules of conduct, nor suffer her name ever again to be mentioned in his presence.

The reverend father compelled her, in atonement for her sins, to sit at a frugal table; to consecrate her vast wealth to objects of benevolence; to wear haircloth next her skin, and around her waist a girdle with sharp points, which lacerated her body at every movement. She was also daily employed in making garments of the coarsest materials with her own hands for the sick in the hospitals, and for the poor in their squalid homes.

The guilty marchioness was dreadfully afraid of death. Every night a careful guard of women watched her bedside. In a thunder-storm she would take an infant in her lap, that the child's innocence might be her protection. In the night of the 26th of May, 1707, she was attacked in her bed by very distressing suffocation. One of her sons, the Marquis of Antin, was immediately sent for. He found his mother insensible. Seizing a casket which contained her jewels, he demanded of an attendant the key. It was suspended around the neck of his dying mother, where she ever wore it. The young man went to the bedside, tore away the lace which veiled his mother's bosom, seized the key, unlocked the casket, emptied its contents into his pockets, descended to his carriage, and hurried away with the treasure, leaving his mother to die without a relative to close her eyes. An hour after she breathed her last.

The king was informed of the death of Madame de Montespan just as he was setting out on a shooting excursion. "Ah! indeed," he said, "and so the marchioness is dead. I should have thought that she would have lasted longer. Are you ready, M. de la Rochefoucald? I have no doubt that after this last shower the scent will lie well for the dogs. Come, let us be off at once."

We have slightly anticipated the chronological sequence of events in this narrative of the death of Madame de Montespan, which took place in the year

1707. James II. of England died in exile at St. Germain in September, 1701. The Prince of Orange then occupied the British throne with the title of William III. He formed what was called the "Grand Alliance" against the encroachments of France. For several years the war of the "Spanish Succession" raged with almost unprecedented fury throughout all Europe.

[Illustration: FRONT VIEW OF ST. GERMAIN.]

The king's health was now failing, and troubles in rapid succession came crowding upon him. His armies encountered terrible defeats. The king had thus far lived on friendly terms with his only brother Philip, duke of Orleans, the playmate of his childhood, and the submissive subject of maturer years. They were now both soured by misfortune. In a chance meeting at Marly they fell into a violent altercation respecting the conduct of one of the sons of the duke. It was their first quarrel since childhood. The duke was so excited by the event that he hastened to his palace at St. Cloud with flushed cheeks and trembling nerves, where he was stricken down by apoplexy. A courier was immediately dispatched to the king. He hastened to the bedside of his brother, and found him insensible.

Philip was two years younger than Louis. To see him die was a louder appeal to the conscience of the king than the view of St. Denis from the terrace at St. Germain. Death was, to this monarch, truly the king of terrors. He could not endure the spectacle of his brother's dying convulsions. Burying his face in his hands, he wept and sobbed bitterly. It was a midnight scene, or rather it was the sombre hour of three o'clock in the morning.

At 8 o'clock in the morning the king took his carriage and returned to Marly, and repaired immediately to the apartment of Madame de Maintenon. At 11 o'clock his physician arrived with the intelligence that the duke was dead. Again the king was overcome with emotion, and wept almost convulsively; but, soon recovering himself, he apparently resolved to make every effort to throw off these painful thoughts.

Notwithstanding the remonstrances of Madame de Maintenon, he persisted in his determination to dine, as usual, with the ladies of the court. Much to the astonishment of the ladies, he was heard, in his own room, singing an air from a recent opera which was far from funereal in its character.

In the month of May of this same year, 1701, the Duke of Anjou, the young

KARTINDO PUBLISHING HOUSE (Kartindo.Com)

King of Spain, who was uneasily seated upon his beleaguered throne, entered into a matrimonial alliance with Maria Louisa of Savoy, younger sister of Adelaide, the duchess of Burgoyne. She was of fairy-like stature, but singularly graceful and beautiful, with the finest complexion, and eyes of dazzling brilliance. Her mental endowments were also equal to her physical charms. Louis XIV., ever anxious to retain the control over the court of Spain, appointed the Princess des Ursins to be the companion and adviser of the young queen. This lady was alike remarkable for her intelligence, her sagacity, her tact, and her thorough acquaintance with high and courtly breeding. The young King of Spain was perfectly enamored of his lovely bride. She held the entire control over him. The worldly-wise and experienced Princess des Ursins guided, in obedience to the dictates of Louis XIV., almost every thought and volition of the young queen. Thus the monarch at Marly ruled the court at Madrid.

While foreign war was introducing bankruptcy to the treasury of France, civil war was also desolating the kingdom. The sufferings of the Protestants equaled any thing which had been witnessed in the days of pagan persecution. The most ferocious of all these men, who were breathing out threatenings and slaughter, was the Abbé de Chayla. This wretch had captured a party of Protestants, and, with them, two young ladies from families of distinction. They were all brutally thrust into a dungeon, and were fettered in a way which caused extreme anguish, and crushed some of their bones. It was the 24th of July, 1702. At ten o'clock in the evening, a party of about fifty resolute Protestants, thoroughly armed, and chanting a psalm, broke into the palace of the infamous ecclesiastic, released the prisoners from the dungeon vaults, seized the abbé, and, after compelling him to look upon the mangled bodies and broken bones of his victims, put him to death by a dagger-stroke from each one of his assailants. The torch was then applied, and the palace laid in ashes.

Hence commenced the terrible civil war called *The War of the Camisards*. The Protestants were poor, dispersed, without arms, and without leaders. Despair nerved them. They fled to rocks, to the swamps, the forests. In their unutterable anguish they were led to frenzies of enthusiasm. They believed that God chose their leaders, and inspired them to action. Thus roused and impelled, they set at defiance an army of twenty thousand men sent against them.

The terrible war lasted two years. Fiends could not have perpetrated greater cruelties than were perpetrated by the troops of the king. It is one of the mysteries of divine providence that *one man* should have been permitted to create such wide-spread and unutterable woe. Louis XIV. wished to exterminate Protestantism from his realms. Millions were made wretched to an intensity which no pen can describe. Louis XIV. wished to place his grandson, without any legal title, upon the throne of Spain. In consequence, Europe was deluged in blood. Cities were sacked and burned. Provinces were devastated. Hundreds of thousands perished in the blood of the battle-field. The book of final judgment alone can tell how many widows and orphans went weeping to their graves.

The Pope Clement IX. fulminated a bull against the Camisards, and promised the absolute remission of sins to those engaged in their extermination. Protestant England and Holland sent words of cheer to their fellow-religionists. We can not enter into the details of this conflict. The result was that the king found it impossible to exterminate the Protestants, or to blot out their faith. A policy of semi-tolerance was gradually introduced, though in various parts of the kingdom the persecuting spirit remained for several years unbroken. The king, chagrined by the failure of his plans, would not allow the word Protestant or Huguenot to be pronounced in his presence.

The distress in France was dreadful. A winter of unprecedented severity had even frozen the impetuous waters of the Rhone. Provisions commanded famine prices. The fields were barren, the store-houses exhausted, the merchant ships were captured by the enemy, and the army, humiliated by frequent defeats, was perishing with hunger. The people became desperate. The king was ignominiously lampooned and placarded. He dared not appear in public, for starving crowds gathered around his carriage clamoring for bread. Even the king and the nobility sent their plate to the Mint. The exhaustion of the realm had become so complete that the haggard features of want seemed to be staring in even at the windows of the palace. Madame de Maintenon practiced so much self-denial as to eat only oaten bread.

In April of 1711 the dauphin was taken sick with apparently an attack of fever. It proved to be malignant smallpox. After a brief sickness, which terrified and dispersed the court, he died, almost alone, in a burning fever, with a frightfully swollen face, and in delirium. Even the king could not visit the dying chamber of his son. He fainted upon his sofa when he heard that the dauphin was in his last agonies.

The terror-stricken courtiers fled from the palace of Meudon, where the loathsome remains of the heir to the throne of France awaited burial. The corpse was hurried into a plain coffin, which was not even covered by the royal pall. Not a single mourning coach followed the only legitimate son of Louis

XIV. to the grave. He had two sisters, the Princess of Conti and the Duchess of Bourbon Condé. Neither of them ventured to join the funeral procession of their only brother. He had three sons, Louis, Philip, and Charles. Philip was king of Spain. Louis and Charles were at home. But they kept at a safe distance, as did the king his father, from the meagre funeral procession which bore, with indecent haste, the remains of the prince to the vaults of St. Denis.

CHAPTER XII

THE LAST DAYS OF LOUIS XIV

1712-1715

The Duke of Burgoyne.--His character.--The dauphiness poisoned by means of snuff.--Anguish of the king.--Death.--The dauphin taken ill.--Death of the dauphin.--Death of the child-dauphin.--The Duke of Orleans.--He is suspected as the poisoner.--A quarrel and its result.--Death of the Duke de Berri.--Anguish of the Duke of Orleans.--Feelings of the king.--The regency.--Intrigues and plots.--Louis harassed.--The Duke of Orleans removes to St. Cloud.--Policy.--Wretchedness of the king.--The Duchess de Berri.--Plottings.--The council of regency.--The last testament of the king.--Unsatisfactory.--Sickness of the king.--The last review.--Struggles against death.--Affects youthfulness.--Summons a band.--Scene in the death-chamber.--The last offices of the Church.--The king resigned.--Remorse of the king.--Energy of fanaticism.--Deplorable condition of France.--Testimony of Thomas Jefferson.--Napoleon.--Devotion of Madame de Maintenon.--Last messages.--Melancholy spectacle.--The young heir to the throne.--Dying advice.--The king blesses the dauphin.--Dying confession.--Scenes of suffering.--Last words.--The death of the king.--Louis XV. proclaimed.--Ignominious burial of Louis XIV.--Louis XV.--Louis XVI.--The Revolution.

Upon the death of the king's son, the Duke of Burgoyne assumed the title of Dauphin, which his father had previously borne, and became direct heir to the crown. He was a retiring, formal man, very much devoted to study, and somewhat pedantic. He was also religiously inclined. In his study, where he passed most of his time, he divided his hours between works of devotion and books of science. His sudden advent to the direct heirship to the French throne surrounded him with courtiers and flatterers. The palace at Meudon, where he generally resided, was now crowded with noble guests.

He became affable, frequently showed himself in public, entered into amusements, and was soon regarded as a general favorite. Taught by Madame de Maintenon, he succeeded, by his marked respect for the king and his submission to his slightest wishes, in gaining the good will of the homage-loving monarch. The years had rolled rapidly along, and the young dauphin was

KARTINDO PUBLISHING HOUSE (Kartindo.Com)

thirty years of age. He had three children, and, being irreproachable in his domestic relations, was developing a very noble character. The dauphiness had attained her twenty-seventh year. She was an extremely beautiful and fascinating woman.

The dauphiness was fond of snuff. On the 3d of February, 1712, the Duke de Noailles, a true friend, presented her with a box of Spanish snuff, with which she was delighted. She left the box upon the table in her boudoir. It was there for a couple of days, she frequently indulging in the luxury of a pinch. On the 5th she was attacked with sudden sickness, accompanied by shivering fits, burning fever, and intense pain in the head. The attack was so sudden and extraordinary that all the attendants thought of poison, though none ventured to give utterance to the surmise. For four days she grew worse, with frequent seasons of delirium. The dauphin was almost frantic. The king sat in anguish, hour after hour, at her bedside.

No remedies were of any avail. Her sufferings were so great that the dauphin could not remain in her dying chamber to witness her agony. She was greatly surprised when informed that she must die. All the offices of the Church were attended to. She received the rite of extreme unction, and, in the wildness of delirium, lost all recognition of those who were around her. The king, bowed down with anguish, was with difficulty prevailed upon to retire. He had but reached the door of the palace when she expired.

The king was now a world-weary, heart-stricken old man, who had numbered more than his threescore years and ten. He seemed crushed with grief, and his eyes were flooded with tears as he returned, with Madame de Maintenon, to Marly. The apartment which the dauphin paced in agony was immediately above the dying chamber. As soon as the death-struggle was over, he was induced to retire to Marly, that he might be spared the anguish of witnessing the preparations for the funeral.

As the dauphin entered the chamber of the king, the monarch was startled in witnessing the change which had taken place in his appearance. His face was flushed with fever; his eyes were dilated and inflamed, and livid stains covered his face. It was manifest that the same disease, whatever it was, which had stricken down the dauphiness, had also attacked the dauphin. The malady made rapid progress. In the intensity of his anguish, the sufferer declared his entrails were on fire. Conscious that his dying hour had come, he, on the night of the 17th, partook of the sacrament of the Lord's Supper, and almost immediately expired.

KARTINDO PUBLISHING HOUSE (Kartindo.Com)

The dreadful tidings were conveyed to the king as he sat in the apartment of Madame de Maintenon, with the younger brother of the dauphin, Charles, the duke de Berri, by his side. The king, anticipating the announcement, sat with his head bent down upon his breast, and clasping almost convulsively the hand of the prince who sat at his feet. Throwing his arms around the neck of the Duke de Berri, the king exclaimed, in accents of despair, "Alas! my son, you alone are now left to me."

The Duke of Burgoyne had buried three children. There were two then living. The eldest, the Duke of Bretagne, was five years of age. The youngest, the Duke of Anjou, had just attained his second year. By the death of the Duke of Burgoyne, his eldest child became the dauphin and the immediate heir to the crown. The next day both of these children were taken sick, evidently with the same malady, whether of natural disease or the effect of poison, which had proved so fatal to their parents. The eldest immediately died. The same funeral car conveyed the remains of the father, the mother, and the child to the gloomy vaults of St. Denis.

The youngest child, the Duke of Anjou, by the most careful nursing recovered to ascend the throne with the title of Louis XV., and to present to the world, in his character, one of the most infamous kings who had ever worn an earthly crown.

We have previously mentioned the death of the king's only brother, Philip, duke of Orleans. He left a son, the Duke of Chartres. Upon the death of the Duke of Orleans his son inherited the title and the estate of his father. He was an exceedingly dissolute man. Should all the legitimate descendants of the king die, he would be heir to the throne. With the exception of Philip, who was King of Spain, and thus precluded from inheriting the throne of France, all were now dead except the infant Duke of Anjou. The death of that child would place the crown upon the brow of Philip, duke of Orleans.

As it was evident that all these victims had died of poison, suspicion was so directed against the Duke of Orleans that the accusation was often hooted at him in the streets. There is, however, no convincing evidence that he was guilty. One of the daughters of the Duke of Orleans had married the Duke de Berri. She was as wicked as she was beautiful, and scarcely condescended to disguise her profligacy. The duke intercepted some letters which proved her guilty intimacy with an officer of her household. A violent quarrel took place in the royal presence. The husband kicked his wife with his heavy boot, and the king lifted his cane to strike the duke.

A sort of reconciliation was effected. The duchess, who, beyond all doubt, was a guilty woman, professed to be satisfied with the apologies which her husband made. Soon after they went on a wolf-hunt in the forest of Marly. Both appeared in high spirits. The run was long. Heated by the race and thirsty, the duke asked the duchess if she had any thing with her with which he could quench his thirst. She drew from the pocket of her carriage a small bottle, which contained, she said, an exquisite cordial with which she was always provided in case of over-fatigue. The duke drained it, and returned the empty bottle to the duchess. As she took it she said, with a smile, "I am very glad to have met you so opportunely."

Thus they parted. In a few hours the duke was a corpse. It was so manifestly for the interest of the dissolute and unprincipled Duke of Orleans that the princes which stood between him and the throne should be removed, that all these cases of poisoning were attributed to him. Indeed, one of the motives which might have influenced his daughter, the Duchess de Berri, to poison her husband, whom she loathed, may have been the hope of seeing her father upon the throne. When the funeral procession passed near the Palais Royal, the residence of the duke, the tumult was so great that it was feared that the palace might be sacked.

The anguish of the duke, thus clamorously assailed with the crime of the most atrocious series of assassinations, was great. A friend, the Marquis de Canillac, calling upon him one day, found him prostrate upon the floor of his apartment in utter despair. He knew that he was suspected by his uncle the king, and by the court as well as by the populace. At last he went boldly to the king, and demanded that he should be arrested, sent to the Bastile, and put upon trial. The king sternly, and without any manifestation of sympathy, refused, saying that such a scandal should not, with his consent, be made any more public than it already was. The king also recoiled from the idea of having a prince of the blood royal tried for murder.

As it was known that the king could not live long, and a babe of but two years was to be his successor--a feeble babe, who had already narrowly escaped death by poison, the question of the regency, during the minority of this babe, and of heirship to the throne in case the babe should die, became a matter of vast moment. The court was filled with intrigues and plots. The Duke of Orleans had his numerous partisans, men of opulence and rank. He was but a nephew of the king--son of the king's brother.

On the other hand was the Duke du Maine, an acknowledged *son* of the king--

the legitimated son of Madame de Montespan. But no royal decree, no act of Parliament could obliterate the stain of his birth. He had many and powerful supporters, who, by his accession to power, would be placed in all the offices of honor and emolument. Madame de Maintenon, in herself a host, was one of the most devoted of his friends. She had been his tutor. She had ever loved him ardently. He had also pledged her, in case of his success, that she should be recognized as Queen of France.

The monarch was harassed and bewildered by these contending factions. The populace took sides. The Duke of Orleans could not leave his palace without being exposed to the hootings of the rabble. He withdrew from his city residence, the Palais Royal, to the splendid palace of St. Cloud. He was accompanied by a magnificent train of nobles, and, being a man of almost boundless wealth, he established his court here in regal splendor.

There was no *proof* that the Duke of Orleans was implicated in the poisonings. The king was unwilling to receive evidence that his brother's son could be guilty of such a crime. Being superstitiously a religionist, the king recoiled from the attempt to place upon the throne a son of Madame de Montespan, who was the acknowledged wife of another man. He therefore favored the claims of the Duke of Orleans, and sent him word at St. Cloud that he recognized his innocence of the crime of which public rumor accused him.

It is, however, very evident that this was a measure of policy and not of sincere conviction. He entered into no friendly relations with the duke, and kept him at a respectful distance. The disastrous war of the Spanish Succession was now closed, through the curious complications of state policy. Philip VI. retained his throne, but France was exhausted and impoverished. The king often sat for hours, with his head leaning upon his hand, in a state of profound listlessness and melancholy. Famine was ravaging the land. A wail of woe came from millions whom his wars and extravagance had reduced to starvation.

The Duchess de Berri, the unblushing profligate, the undoubted murderess, was, as the daughter of the king's brother, the only legitimate princess left to preside over the royal court. She was fascinating in person and manners, with scarcely a redeeming virtue to atone for her undisguised vices.

"Thus the stately court of Anne of Austria, the punctilious circle of Maria Theresa, and the elegant society of the Duchess of Burgoyne were--at the very period of his life when Louis XIV., at length disenchanted of the greatness, and disgusted with the vices of the world, was seeking to purify his heart and to exalt his thoughts that they might become more meet for heaven--superseded by the orgies of a wanton, who, with unabashed brow and unshrinking eye, carried her intrigues into the very saloons of Marly."[Y]

[Footnote Y: Louis XIV. and the Court of France, vol. ii., p. 588.]

Madame de Maintenon resorted to every measure she could devise to induce the king to appoint her favorite pupil, the Duke du Maine, regent during the minority of the infant Duke of Anjou. The king was greatly harassed. Old, infirm, world-weary, heart-stricken, and pulled in opposite directions, by powers so strong, he knew not what to do. At last he adopted a sort of compromise, which gave satisfaction to neither party.

The king appointed a council of regency, of which the Duke of Orleans was president. But the Duke du Maine was a member of the council, and was also intrusted with the guardianship and education of the young heir to the throne. This will was carefully concealed in a cavity opened in the wall of a tower of the state apartment. The iron door of this closet was protected by three keys, one of which was held by the president of the chambers, one by the attorney general, and one by the public registrar.

A royal edict forbade the closet to be opened until after the death of the king, and then only in the presence of the assembled Parliament, the princes, and the peers. The document had been extorted from the king. It was not in accordance with his wishes. Indeed, it satisfied no one. As he placed the papers in the hands of the president of the chambers, he said to him, gloomily,

"Here is my will. The experience of my predecessors has taught me that it may not be respected. But I have been tormented to frame it. I have been allowed neither peace nor rest until I complied. Take it away. Whatever may happen to it, I hope that I shall now be left in quiet."[Z]

[Footnote Z: Memoires de St. Simon.]

The advanced age of the king and his many infirmities rendered even a slight indisposition alarming. On the evening of the 3d of May, 1715, the king, having supped with the Duchess de Berri, retired to bed early, complaining of weariness and exhaustion. The rumor spread rapidly that the king was dangerously sick. The foreign embassadors promptly dispatched the news to their several courts.

The jealous king, who kept himself minutely informed of every thing which transpired, was very indignant in view of this apparent eagerness to hurry him to the tomb. To prove, not only to the court, but to all Europe, that he was still every inch a king, he ordered a magnificent review of the royal troops at Marly. The trumpet of preparation was blown loudly. Many came, not only from different parts of the kingdom, but from the other states of Europe, to witness the spectacle. It took place on the 20th of June, 1715. As the troops, in their gorgeous uniforms, defiled before the terrace of Marly, quite a spruce-looking man, surrounded by obsequious attendants, emerged from the principal entrance of the palace, descended the marble steps and mounted his horse. It was the poor old king. Inspired by vanity, which even dying convulsions could not quell, he had rouged his pale and haggard cheeks, wigged his thin locks, padded his skeleton limbs, and dressed himself in the almost juvenile costume of earlier years. Sustained by artificial stimulants, this poor old man kept his tottering seat upon his saddle for four long hours. He then, having proved that he was still young and vigorous, returned to his chamber. The wig was thrown aside, the pads removed, the paint washed off, and the infirm septuagenarian sought rest from his exhaustion upon the royal couch.

Day after day the king grew more feeble, with the usual alternations of nervous strength and debility, but with no abatement of his chronic gloom. The struggles which he endured to conceal the approaches of decay did but accelerate that decay. He was restless, and again lethargic. Dropsical symptoms appeared in his discolored feet and swollen ankles. Still he insisted every day upon seeing his ministers, and exhibited himself padded, and rouged, and costumed in the highest style of art. He even affected, in his gait and gesture, the elasticity of youth. In his restlessness, the king repaired, with his court, from Marly to Versailles.

Here the king was again taken seriously sick with an attack of fever. With unabated resolution, he continued his struggles against the approaches of the angel of death. While the fevered blood was throbbing in his veins, he declared that he was but slightly indisposed, and summoned a musical band to his presence, with orders that the musicians should perform only the most animating and cheerful melodies.

But the fever and other alarming symptoms increased so rapidly that scarcely had the band been assembled when the court physicians became apprehensive that the king's dissolution was immediately to take place. The king's confessor and the Cardinal de Rohan were promptly summoned to attend to the last services of the Catholic Church for the dying. There was a scene of confusion in the palace. The confessor, Le Tellier, communicated to the king the intelligence that he was probably near his end. While he was receiving the *confession* of the royal penitent, the cardinal was hurrying to the chapel to get the viaticum for administering the communion, and the holy oil for the rite of extreme unction.

It was customary that the *pyx*, as the box was called in which the host was kept, should be conveyed to the bedside of expiring royalty in formal procession. The cardinal, in his robes of office, led the way. Several attendants of the royal household followed, bearing torches. Then came Madame de Maintenon. They all gathered in the magnificent chamber, and around the massive, sumptuous couch of the monarch. The cardinal, after speaking a few words in reference to the solemnity of a dying hour, administered the sacrament and the holy oils. The king listened reverently and in silence, and then sank back upon his pillow, apparently resigned to die.

To the surprise of all, he revived. Patiently he bore his sufferings, which at times were severe. His legs began to swell badly and painfully. Mortification took place. He was informed that the amputation of the leg was necessary to save him from speedy death.

"Will the operation prolong my life?" inquired the king.

"Yes, sire," the surgeon replied; "certainly for some days, perhaps for several weeks."

"If that be all," said the king, "it is not worth the suffering. God's will be done."

The king could not conceal the anguish with which he was agitated in view of his wicked life. He fully believed in the religion of the New Testament, and that after death came the judgment. He tried to believe that the priest had power to grant him absolution from his sins. How far he succeeded in this no one can know.

Openly he expressed his anguish in view of the profligacy of his youth, and wept bitterly in the retrospect of those excesses. We know not what compunctions of conscience visited him as he reflected upon the misery he had caused by the persecution of the Protestants. But he had been urged to this by his highest ecclesiastics, and even by the holy father himself.

It would not be strange, under these circumstances, if a man of his superstitious and fanatical spirit should, even in a dying hour, reflect with some complacency upon these crimes, believing that thus he had been doing God service. It is this which gives to papal *fanaticism* its terrible and demoniac energy. The *sincere* papist believes "*heresy*" to be poison for the soul infinitely more dreadful than any poison for the body. Such poison must be banished from the world at whatever cost of suffering. Many an ecclesiastic has gone from his closet of prayer to kindle the flames which consumed his victim. The more *sincere* the papist is in his belief, the more mercilessly will he swing the scourge and fire the fagot.

Loudly, however, he deplored the madness of his ambition which had involved Europe in such desolating wars. Bitterly he expressed his regret that he left France in a state of such exhaustion, impoverished, burdened with taxation, and hopelessly crushed by debt.

The condition of the realm was indeed deplorable. A boy of five years of age was to inherit the throne. A man so profligate that he was infamous even in a court which rivaled Sodom in its corruption was to be invested with the regency of the kingdom--a man who was accused, by the general voice of the nation, of having poisoned those who stood between him and the throne. That man's sister, an unblushing wanton, who had poisoned her own husband, presided over the festivities of the palace. The nobles, abandoned to sensual indulgence, were diligent and ingenious only in their endeavors to wrench money from the poor. The masses of the people were wretched beyond description, and almost beyond imagination in our land of liberty and competence. The execrations of the starving millions were rising in a long wail around the throne.

Thomas Jefferson, subsequently President of the United States, who, not many years after this, was the American embassador at Paris, wrote, in 1785, to Mrs. Trist, of Philadelphia,

"Of twenty millions of people supposed to be in France, I am of the opinion that there are nineteen millions more wretched, more accursed in every circumstance of human existence than the most conspicuously wretched individual of the whole United States."

KARTINDO PUBLISHING HOUSE (Kartindo.Com)

Even the Duke of Orleans, the appointed regent, said, "If I were a subject I would certainly revolt. The people are good-natured fools to suffer so long."

These sufferings and these corruptions were the origin and cause of the French Revolution.[AA] Napoleon, the great advocate of the rights of the people in antagonism to this aristocratic privilege, said, at St. Helena,

[Footnote AA: Abbott's French Revolution, as viewed in the Light of Republican Institutions.]

"Our Revolution was a national convulsion as irresistible in its effects as an eruption of Vesuvius. When the mysterious fusion which takes place in the entrails of the earth is at such a crisis that an explosion follows, the eruption bursts forth. The unperceived workings of the discontent of the people follow exactly the same course. In France, the sufferings of the people, the moral combinations which produce a revolution, had arrived at maturity, and the explosion took place."[AB]

[Footnote AB: Napoleon at St. Helena, p. 374]

Such was the condition in which unhappy France was left by Louis XIV., after a reign of seventy years. He was now seventy-seven years of age. Madame de Maintenon, two years his senior, was entering her eightieth year. With unwearied devotion she watched at the bedside of that selfish husband whose pride would never allow him to acknowledge her publicly as his wife.

Feeling that his end was drawing near, the king summoned the Duke of Orleans to his bedside, and informed him minutely of the measures he wished to have adopted after his death. The duke listened respectfully, but paid no more regard to the wishes of the now powerless and dying king than to the wailing of the wind. The king had penetration enough to see that his day was over. He sank back upon his pillow in despair.

On the 26th of August several prominent members of his court were invited to the dying chamber of the king. His voice was almost gone. He beckoned them to gather near around his bed. Then, in feeble tones, tremulous with emotion, the pitiable old man, conscious of his summons to the tribunal of God, said,

"Gentlemen, I ask your pardon for the bad example I have set you. I thank you for your fidelity to me, and beg you to be equally faithful to my grandson. Farewell, gentlemen. Forgive me. I hope you will sometimes think of me when I am gone."

"By many a death-bed I have been, By many a sinner's parting scene, But never aught like this."

It was, indeed, a spectacle mournfully sublime. The dying chamber was one of the most magnificent apartments in the palace of Versailles. The royal couch, massive in its architecture, richly curtained in its embroidered upholstery of satin and gold, presented a bed whose pillowed luxury exhibited haggard death in the strongest possible contrast.

Upon this gorgeous bed the gray-haired king reclined, wrinkled and wan, and with a countenance which bore the traces both of physical suffering and of keen remorse. The velvet hangings of the bed were looped back with heavy tassels of gold. A group of nobles in gorgeous court costumes were kneeling around the bed. Dispersed over the vast apartment were other groups of courtiers and ladies, in picturesque attitudes of real or affected grief. The gilded cornices, the richly-painted ceilings, the soft carpet, yielding to the pressure of the foot, the lavish display of the most costly and luxurious furniture, all conspired to render the dimmed eye, and wasted cheek, and palsied frame of the dying more impressive.

At a gesture from the king nearly all retired. For a few moments there was unbroken silence. The king then requested his great grandchild, who was to be his successor, to be brought to him. A cushion was placed by the side of the bed, and the half-frightened child, clinging to the hand of his governess, kneeled upon it. Louis XIV. gazed for a few moments with almost pitying tenderness upon the infant prince, and then said,

"My child, you are about to become a great king. Do not imitate me either in my taste for building or in my love of war. Live in peace with the nations. Render to God all that you owe him. Teach your subjects to honor His name. Strive to relieve the burdens of your people, in which I have been so unfortunate as to fail. Never forget the gratitude you owe to the Duchess de Ventadour."[AC]

[Footnote AC: The Duchess de Ventadour, by the most careful nursing, to which she entirely devoted herself, had rescued the infant Duke of Anjou from the effect of the poison to which his father, mother, and brother had fallen victims.]

"Madame," said the king, addressing Madame de Ventadour, "permit me to embrace the prince."

The dauphin was placed upon the bed. The king encircled him in his arms, pressed him fondly to his breast, and said, in a voice broken by emotion,

"I bless you, my dear child, with all my heart." He then raised his eyes to heaven, and uttered a short prayer for God's blessing upon the boy.

The next day, after another night of languor and suffering, the restless, conscience-stricken king again summoned the dignitaries of the court to his bedside, and said to them, in the presence of Madame de Maintenon and of his *confessor*, who had mainly instigated him in the persecution of the Protestants,

"Gentlemen, I die in the faith and obedience of the Church. I know nothing of the dogmas by which it is divided. I have followed the advice which I have received, and have done only what I was desired to do. If I have erred, my guides alone must answer before God, whom I call upon to witness this assertion."

The succeeding night the king was restless and greatly agitated. He could not sleep, and seemed to pass the whole night in agonizing prayer. In the morning he said to Madame de Maintenon,

"At this moment I only regret yourself. I have not made you happy. But I have ever felt for you all the regard and affection which you deserved. My only consolation in leaving you exists in the hope that we shall, ere long, meet again in eternity."

Hours of agony, bodily and mental, were still allotted to the king. His limbs were badly swollen. Upon one of them mortification was rapidly advancing. He was often delirious, with but brief intervals of consciousness. The service for the dying was performed. The ceremony seemed slightly to arouse him from his lethargy. His voice was heard occasionally blending with the prayers of the ecclesiastics as he repeated several times,

"Now, in the hour of death, O my God, come to my aid."

These were his last words. He sank back insensible upon his pillow. A few hours of painful breathing passed away, and at eight o'clock in the morning of the 1st of September, 1715, he expired, in the seventy-seventh year of his age and the seventy-second of his reign. It was the longest reign in the annals of France. Had he been governed through this period by enlightened Christian principle, how many millions might have been made happy whom his crimes doomed to life-long woe!

An immense concourse was assembled in the court-yard at Versailles, anticipating the announcement of his death. The moment he breathed his last sigh, the captain of the body-guard approached the great balcony, threw open the massive windows, and, looking down upon the multitude below, raised his truncheon above his head, broke it in the centre, threw the fragments down into the court-yard, and cried sadly, "The king is dead!"

Then, instantly seizing another staff from the hands of an attendant, he waved it joyfully above his head, and shouted triumphantly, "Long live the king, Louis XV.!" A huzza burst from the lips of the assembled thousands almost loud enough to pierce the ear of the king, now palsied in death.

There were few to mourn the departed monarch. As his remains were hurried to the vaults of St. Denis, those vaults which he had so much dreaded, the populace shouted execrations and pelted his coffin with mud. Not the slightest regard was paid to his will. The Duke of Orleans assumed the regency with absolute power. His reign was execrable, followed by the still more infamous reign of Louis XV. Then came the Revolution, as the sceptre of utterly despotic sway passed into the hands of the feeble Louis XVI. The storm, which had been gathering for ages, burst with fury which appalled the world. A more tremendous event has not occurred in the history of our race. The story has too often been told by those who were in sympathy with the kings and the nobles. The time will come when the *people's* side of the story will be received, and the terrible drama will be better understood.

THE END

KARTINDO PUBLISHING HOUSE (Kartindo.Com)

www.ingramcontent.com/pod-product-compliance
Lightning Source LLC
Chambersburg PA
CBHW060508290526
45791CB00001B/314